FARMING *with* NATURE

FARMING with NATURE

by JOSEPH A. COCANNOUER

NORMAN : UNIVERSITY OF OKLAHOMA PRESS

Books by Joseph A. Cocannouer

Trampling out the Vintage (Norman, 1945)
Weeds: Guardians of the Soil (New York, 1948)
Farming with Nature (Norman, 1954)

Library of Congress Catalog Card Number: 54–5935

A PATHFINDER BOOK REPRINT EDITION
Complete and Unabridged

Printed in the United States of America

ISBN: 979-8869094155

To Mary Eugenia Stith
A Very Efficient and
Painstaking Editor

Foreword

FEW words in any civilized language are used less correctly than is the word *nature*. We are exalted by the beauties of earth and sky—a crimson sunset, a flower-decked meadow, the majesty of a snow-capped mountain. The emotionally inclined go into ecstasies over the prismatic colors in a rainbow and sigh romantically over a snowy landscape in the moonlight. And we call these pictures Nature, whereas they are but the manifestations of Nature. Nature is the law back of the manifestations; the principle that maintains rhythm throughout the universe.

A fertile soil is Nature in superb manifestation. It is here that the universal rhythm is at its best. Productive land is a living workshop where many agents are on the job preparing ingredients, though inadvertently, to be used by growing plants in building complete foods, not only for themselves but for the animal kingdom as well. As goes this workshop of the soil, so goes humankind on the earth. Indeed, all organic life is completely at the mercy of the processes going on in the soil's workshop. The fact that plants secure the greater portion of their nutrients from the air in no wise lessens the value of the nutrients derived from the soil. Without the latter, there would be no life on the earth as we know it.

I like to think of this soil-world as a chain made up of numerous fertility links. Each of these links, operating under the mandates of Nature, performs a series of specific tasks as a part of one harmonious whole. Though some of these fertility links would appear to be more essential than others in supporting organic life on the earth, the fact of the matter is—all are indispensables. From the standpoint of the farmer, though, some of the links that make up this marvelous chain are more vital than others, simply because they are within the farmer's power to control them. That is, through his land operations the farmer can either strengthen his fertility chain or he can wreck it almost completely by means of incorrect tillage practices.

Consequently, good farming, whether that be understood as the growing of one plant in a pot or the cultivation of vast acreage, consists largely of maintaining an unbroken, dynamic fertility chain in the land. The wise farmer or gardener will seek to understand each one of those fertility links individually; then he will strive to get the most out of them—without violating the natural laws which rule both him and the land which gives him his food. And this is FARMING WITH NATURE.

JOSEPH A. COCANNOUER

Wilburton, Oklahoma
January 20, 1954

Table of Contents

FARMING *with* NATURE

1

Nature at Work

MAN may sense but he probably never will discover the secret of organic life. Nature in her wisdom will not grant to man that last revelation, for to do so would mean man's annihilation. Nature never destroys; she ever constructs.

To build and maintain a complete soil, a soil with an actively functioning fertility chain, is one of Nature's greatest self-assigned tasks. Yet, strangely enough, Nature as a rule does not reach her goal. But it is in soil building that Nature not only reveals herself at work but supplies the wisdom which is absolutely essential to the sustenance of that life the absolute comprehension of which she withholds from us. That is why no knowledge is more vital to man's well-being than a knowledge of the soil which supports him. Or more specifically, a knowledge of the soil's workshop, with which every tiller of the soil must deal intimately.

The evolution of plant growth on the earth is a vital segment of Nature's law governing soil formation and soil maintenance. A diversification of plant roots occupying the same soil area, along with the diversification in the vegetation above ground, with the roots having different demands and different modes of operation, has much to do with maintaining an unbroken fertility chain in productive land. Each root system adds something a bit different from the rest to the sum total of values, thus playing its highly important part in maintaining rhythm in the soil.

This principle is at work all around us, but not always so obviously as it formerly operated on our Great Plains during the period of the bison. This period offers an interesting episode in the history of soils. For many centuries countless thousands of buffalo thrived on the plains. The ability of the grassland to support these vast herds seems to have been possible largely because of the ecological changes in plant growth that occurred there periodically across the centuries. The shifting of plant families, brought about because of overgrazing, prevented soil depletion. Whenever the grass of the plains succumbed, an assortment of hardy weeds moved in immediately and started the reconditioning of the soil for the ultimate return of the grass. The seeds of the grasses were always there, alive but dormant, waiting for suitable sprouting and growing conditions to start them to work in rebuilding the green carpet.

The deep-rooted weeds, many of them not edible by the hungry bison and antelope, though they probably possessed the essential protein for building husky frames and muscles, tapped the rich subsoil and thereby assured a replenishment of the nutrients near the surface, a condition necessary for the growth of thick grass. With the weed roots not only restoring the minerals and nitrates in the surface soil, but also strengthening the soil-sponge, the other indispensable links, the bacteria, the molds, and the earthworms returned to their ageless jobs of rebuilding a suitable environment for the shallow-feeding grass roots. Even when the bison consumed the stems and leaves of the weeds completely, the upward movement of capillary water, which goes on continuously on the *outside* of growing weed roots, brought back to the surface great quantities of the required nutrients. And this system of soil maintenance continued until the white man moved in. Whether the soils on the plains ever reached complete balance is questionable. The drain on them was terrific and the pounding of hoofs relentless. But they had to be potentially good soils to withstand the rough treatment they got, and a rich subsoil storehouse, with weeds and other deep-rooted plants drawing nutrients out of that storehouse, was the main source of strength.

It is possible to maintain an unbroken fertility chain only when the adverse factors in or on the soil do not dominate the situation. Anything that persistently disturbs the surface of the land disrupts Nature's soil-maintenance cycle. Destructive floods, destructive fires, and ravaging man—all of them seriously hamper the constructive natural process, and when they all work together, soil-depletion is inevitable. Most virgin soils are out of balance because something is forever preventing the realization of optimum conditions. But even these disturbances are part of the natural process, necessary in ways that we do not always understand.

Superficial evidence can reveal much of the soil's worth as well as its history, but that evidence means nothing to one who is not able to read the vegetation on such land intelligently. That the plant reveals unmistakably the relative fertility of the soil that supports it, was an adage even among the ancients. To be able to interpret the soil through the plant is agricultural knowledge of the highest order.

Repeating, there are not many regions of the world where a dynamic natural soil exists. Good soils are not uncommon, but superior soils are an exception because of the constantly recurring interferences with Nature and her work on the soil's surface—interference with the building of the vegetative mulch which is necessary in maintaining correct fiberization in land. Without this sponge there is always more or less discord throughout the entire soil world. And any disturbance whatever in the soil's workshop weakens the fertility chain to some extent.

How does one recognize a naturally balanced soil? How can one know a soil where all the links of the fertility chain are strong and functioning satisfactorily? The signs are definite. Fertile soils radiate their completeness in a lush growth, for one thing; vegetation there is characterized by plants fairly vibrating health despite their struggle for existence. Then there are the more subtle signs, the soil's *special manifestations* in stem and leaf and flowers. These less obvious indicators are not so readily detected by the casual naturalist. Yet they can be learned by anyone who has eyes with which to see and who will put them to work when in a forest or field or meadow. Healthy vegetation reveals itself from the roots to the highest terminal bud, revealing in turn a healthy soil below.

A chemical analysis of soil, infinitely valuable though it is, still does not give anything resembling a complete picture of the soil's worth, for chemistry deals primarily with the dead, not the living. Active biology, though, helps greatly to fill out a reliable chart of information. A naturally rich soil is so alive it seems to move when you hold it in your hand. Then there are the rich aromas produced by organic decay and microbes and molds. The latter are unmistakably indicative, whether emerging from a healthy soil itself or from the healthy growth that springs from such soil. The feel of soil can also be a reliable gauge of the soil's richness. One does not forget the touch of highly fertile earth which is dark, crumbly, non-caking when wet. Working in a soil with all of these natural attributes brings one very close to the true potentials for plant growth. And perhaps the best part of this learning process is that one before long finds himself almost unconsciously associating most of the plants he contacts with some particular soil.

As soil regions differ, so also do plant regions differ. The soils of our semi-arid Southwest have been called Nature's magic land because of their quick response when brought under cultivation. This arises from the fact that soil formation goes on to a degree, and continuously, even in a waterless desert. Chemistry is ever at work there, changing the primitive earth substances into usable forms, just as if vegetation were present to utilize the processed materials. Wherever there is the slightest rainfall (and few are the regions in our own country where no moisture at all reaches the soil from the sky), some forms of biological life are there and at work on their soil-forming tasks. Bit by bit across the decades, even centuries, quantities of growth materials are built up because there are few forces present to deplete them. There is little waste of the substances once the microbes are through with them, for no leaching takes place to carry the materials down into and through the fiberless subsoil, and little run-off to carry them completely away. Actually the subsoils in an arid climate are just the reverse of what they are in a humid region. The latter subsoils are strong, as a rule, while desert subsoils are weak. Though the organic content of desert soils is extremely low, all other materials (particularly minerals) are so strong in the surface layer that vegetation leaps into growth once moisture and temperature are adequate to normal plant growth.

Incorrect irrigation practices can cause in a short time serious injury to semi-arid land that has been turned to cultivation. This has happened in Arizona and California as well as in other Western States. Without the organic materials to hold them, the primitive soil nutrients vanish like water through a sieve. Some of these nutrients are held in the subsoil despite the complete absence of a soil sponge, and can be retrieved later, to a considerable extent, through correct land management. Much fertility, however, is lost via the irrigation ditches.

When semi-arid land is brought under cultivation, the

very first move of the farmer should be to build the best possible sponge structure in his soil with green manures or some other organic applications. He will need to fill his new subsoil with reserve nutrients such as are found normally in most humid soils, but he can't do this very extensively until he establishes a subsoil sponge. On new land the farmer should hold his irrigation to the very minimum necessary to produce a reasonable crop. Thousands of acres of good land have been weakened seriously through over-irrigation before the new land was properly conditioned to receive the water. In no place is the soil sponge more vital than in irrigated regions, not to check floods and erosion, but to prevent the loss of plant nutrients. Pouring water onto land simply because water is plentiful will in the long run prove to be the worst kind of land management.

Whether in a humid region or in a region dependent upon irrigation, the same soil laws govern, taking the form of organic strength which guarantees a vigorous force of microbes, molds, algae, and earthworms; and a subsoil storehouse rich in minerals and nitrates. Until these conditions obtain in cultivated land, the harvests will fall short in both quality and quantity.

Despite the fact that perfect soils are not common in the natural world, as has already been pointed out, Nature does reach her goal now and then, and, like as not, where one would least expect it. There is no adventure more thrilling or more instructive than to study soil-building, as it actually takes place. And for such a study nothing can surpass a badly eroded field—a really sick field. There, if one is closely observant, he may for the first time learn the true meaning of persistence. Even more, he should discover to his complete satisfaction that Nature never accepts defeat. It may take considerable exploring before the explorer's eyes begin to pick up those spots which, when examined carefully, actually prove to be tiny oases in a drab landscape. In time these little oases of living land will bob right out of what at first seemed the worst sort of desolation. A little patience is all one needs to find them. It is then that one begins to see the almost incredible vitality of soil and plants and the materials that bring them to fruition.

Man may destroy. He may leave the door wide open to sweeping floods and sheet erosion. He may invite dust laden winds to come in and carry away the loose earth in clouds. But the little oases which resist the worst of maltreatment will still remain. Maybe it will be some cove particularly sheltered; or a favored niche back of some assemblage of rocks; or a clump of healthy weeds at the head of a swale. Pathetically meager they all are, yet sparks of life that will ultimately develop into exuberant growth and verdant expanse—for that is the law.

But if one aspires to discover just *how* Nature carries on her complete soil-building and soil-maintenance operations, let him search out one of those favored spots of land where Nature has been able to operate unmolested for a long stretch of years. In all regions of normal rainfall these spots can be found, and the very best proof of their existence is the fact that they are inconspicuous. They have been able to survive because they have long been outside man's destructive paths. Maybe it will be a grass patch that has been permitted to go its own way, free from erosion or fire or the activities of man, for longer than anyone can remember.

If one has any love at all for rich earth, once he locates one of those favored spots his first urge will be to start digging; to delve into the soil's depths. And he will need to do considerable digging, for most of the lessons of soil development have to be read below the surface. The surface must not be neglected, though, for it is from the organic mulch that the land draws its materials for fiberizing the soil below. Here, really, is the key to the entire process. Where this mulch does not exist Nature's soil laws cannot operate completely.

The organic process, seemingly simple, is yet complex. The surface mulch consists of leaves and broken stems, put down layer upon layer as the seasons pass. As the bottom layer of the mulch disintegrates into the fiber stage, and then works farther down with the help of earthworms and other animals, a new layer is spread upon the mulch above. It is possible to observe these several stages of decay: the coarse materials above ground, below them the fibers which make up the sponge, then the mellow final product. This change from the coarse materials to the final food ingredients in solution is a slow one, under some conditions requiring several years for the microbes and other soil agents to complete the task. So, when erosion is permitted to do its destructive work, one wonders if the old aphorism isn't more than true: "What Nature builds in centuries, man destroys in days."

Farming with Nature calls for one paramount aim: to build soils to a complete balance in the shortest possible time, something Nature working alone is rarely able to do. However, to build successfully *with* Nature, we need to have a fairly clear understanding of what constitutes Nature's blueprints. True, modern farming methods do not always permit complete adherence to Nature's rules of soil building. On the other hand, there is no type of farming which does not allow a reasonably close approach to it. The farmer has numerous ways of putting the sponge into the soil, and some of these methods will be treated completely in future chapters. A good sponge is essential, for when this spongy condition reaches to a considerable depth, a condition for best crop production is established.

Very little of the lower soil fiber, however, comes from the surface mulch. The major portion of these deeper organic threads is carried down into the soil by insects and earthworms, or is put there by plant roots. With this lower fiberization, brought about in practical land management through the incorporation into the soil of green manures, through sheet composting, or by applying animal manures and crop refuse, several advantages are secured. Not only is the feeding zone for crops enlarged in a natural manner, but there is established a water reservoir which serves as a source of moisture during dry periods. And no less important, a highway is built down to the food storehouse in the subsoil. With earthworms on the job and with deep-rooted weeds or vigorous-rooted domestic crops employed periodically in the rotation, the contents of the subsoil storehouse are being continuously lifted back to the surface; they are kept in rotation.

Farmers and gardeners as a rule ignore their reserves in the subsoil. Without a continuous flow of materials from this reserve up to the surface, normal crop growth is restricted, no matter what soil foods may be added from the outside. No tiller of the soil is completely aware of his soil's needs until he becomes subsoil conscious.

Although few soil observers have discovered it, rich soils reveal themselves best on balmy growing nights. It is then that the many agents of the soil's development are in vigorous action. When the moon is full and there is little or no wind, it is as if the stillness is a sign for an awakening on and all through the surface soil. At night Nature seems to open many doors that are at other times closed. This is revealed by the richer aromas, which indicate the activities of the microbes and molds. Earthworms come to the surface then, and if one will give their movements close study he will be inclined to agree with Charles Darwin that "Those homely worms possess superior intelligence." The rove beetles and ground beetles are active, too. Though they are normally above-the-ground travelers, part of the life-cycle of these beneficial insects is spent down in the earth.

There is a rhythm, an almost audible hum in this activity. What we cannot see, we sense; what we cannot hear, we feel. The natural process, in favorable soil conditions, is prodigious. It can be observed with the microscope, and it can be analyzed in the laboratory, but these methods, while they give us data, sometimes deny us the full truth. Here the process is bigger than its parts, it is slow moving, it avoids extremes, it thrives upon slow moisture absorption, decay, the ceaseless activity of soil acids and bases, soil bacteria, protozoa, and worms and roots. The absence of infinitely small traces of certain minerals in the soil can wreck the rhythm of things, and the absence of other essentials can produce a desert where a natural garden once was.

But to grow mystical about the soil process is to miss a fine natural chemistry and a physical process which, like any other natural phenomena, merely are. Studying them enables man to do as well as Nature, often better.

Let it be said here that I am not one of those who place all of their faith in one creed. As Selman A. Waksman, a Nobel prize winner and one of the greatest of American scientists, has pointed out, the whole soil process is at base scientific, and to endow the organic factor with all the virtues and to build up dogmatic but unsupported statements about it is to fall into errors as old as the beginnings of agriculture.

People, he tells us, "confuse conditions of humus formation in peat bogs with those in mineral and well-aerated soils. This is illustrated by the statement, 'In humus the essential factor is its condition.' This is true, but only to a certain extent. The process of decomposition of plant and animal residues leading to humus formation is highly important in making the soil fertile, since the continuous stream of carbon dioxide, ammonia and nitrate, and phosphate resulting from such decomposition is highly important for continuous plant growth."

From a scientific point of view, however, this does not mean that only the natural process can effect the gains we search for. "It is being argued," Dr. Waksman says, "that use of mineral fertilizers unfavorably influences the chemical composition of plants and their nutritive properties for human and animal consumption. There is accumulating evidence, however, that plants grown in soil enriched with inorganic fertilizers, or in sand supplied with a balanced nutrient solution, including ammonium salts, nitrates, phosphates, potassium salts, and the necessary rare elements, differ very little either in chemical composition or in nutritive properties, from plants grown in natural soil receiving only stable manures or composts."

On the other hand, it is quite clear from man's experience and from experiments conducted in the past half-century that chemicals are not the principal answer to the fertility dilemma. Says Dr. Waksman: "The continuous use of mineral fertilizers on the same soil for many years, without the use of organic manures or growth of sod crops to replace the organic matter lost by clean cultivation, may lead to deterioration of the physical condition of the soil and loss of productivity."

To this I would add that, even if a "natural" soil had the principal elements required in plant growth, and lacked the organic matter required by Nature, it would fail. One of the most important factors here, obviously, is the physical properties of the soil, which natural organic decay or man's substitution or improvement upon it alone can provide.

2

Man Moves In

WHEN man enters the soil-building picture; when he starts out to re-establish rhythm in his land, he has it in his power to operate in a constructive manner, or he can completely disorganize his soil's workshop to his ultimate loss. Co-operation with Nature means just that—CO-OPERATION. Which is to say, in Nature farming the farmer accepts the blueprints of Nature as his guide.

Consequently, here again is Nature's basic soil law: some vegetative mulch which prevents crusting of the soil's surface and which, as it decays, provides sponge-making fiber and food for the microbes in the soil's workshop below; a sponge structure reaching down to considerable depth; and a highway connecting the upper soil layer with the subsoil storehouse. These are the fundamentals of an active fertility chain. In cultivated land the sponge must of course be maintained through the farmer's *application* of the necessary organic substances. Furthermore, the farmer has to accept what Nature gives him in the way of a subsoil. But by sticking close to Nature he can in many cases bring back to the surface much valuable material, even from the weaker subsoils.

Applying materials from the outside in order to maintain soil fertility in heavily cropped land is a necessity. This is doubly true when soil has dropped to a very low ebb through over-cropping or general neglect. If left undisturbed for a long period of years, Nature will repair the fertility chain in the worst of soils. But with man time is a factor; man cannot wait on Nature's slow processes. Fortunately Nature permits a shortening of her operations to a considerable extent, and it is just here that scientific co-operation with Nature can really be made to count.

While the inorganics—the powdered rocks—were actually the beginning of soil on the earth, the core of productive land is its organic content. This does not mean that the mineral nutrients per se are not equally essential to plant growth, but rather that, for the harmonious functioning of all the elements, animate and inanimate, that are directly responsible for a soil's productiveness, there must be an abundance of plant material in several stages of decay. It is important to keep in mind that when the organic content of the soil is strong, there is far less danger of disturbing microorganisms when quick-acting materials are added from outside than when the organics are weak. The soil sponge serves as a balancer.

Farmers will often have to supply extra minerals to their lands even when there is an abundance of minerals in the subsoil storehouse. The subsoil minerals will continue to be largely unavailable until the soil reaches that condition where there is continuous mineral circulation between the upper and lower soils. This latter condition will obtain only when earthworms and deep-rooted weeds or deep-rooted domestic crops are recognized by the farmer as essentials and effectively put to work. A light application of lime will usually be necessary at the start of a land-improving project, as will some form of phosphate. In many regions a treatment of potash will also be needed. No matter what types of commercial fertilizers a farmer may choose to employ, the soil's sponge structure should be built up as quickly as possible so that Nature's own workers can move in in force.

Today we are hearing much about compost as a means of building up and maintaining soil fertility. Compost is nothing more nor less than a natural plant food of high quality, built from plants and plant materials of all sorts much as Nature does it in her primitive forests and meadows. Building truly scientific compost is man-Nature cooperation as it should be. Here we have a fine illustration of how man, utilizing a natural process, can construct plant food surpassing Nature's best and in a mere fraction of the time required when Nature has to do the job alone. Although organic practices were known earlier, the Roman agricultural scientists seem to have been the first to formalize this means of duplicating and speeding up a natural process in maintaining the productiveness of their farmland. Compost making was a must on every Roman farm long before the advent of the Christian era. The Chinese also have been persistent compost builders as far back as their history records.

This employing of plant and animal structures for re-use in the growth processes of plants conforms to a fundamental law of Nature. In his building of compost man is merely short-cutting the life cycle of plants to gain time. His compost materials have already traveled the road of early life and growth, but he usually makes use of them before the normal period of death arrives. To be convinced that composting has Nature's complete approval, one has only to study plant growth on soil that has been fed compost scientifically made.

In order to understand just why compost is a superior soil food, one needs to know, first of all, considerable about those vital ingredients which go into compost making. Since the materials are largely plants or the products from plants, a knowledge of the plant, its growth habits, and so on makes it possible to evaluate the composted product more intelligently. People who make light of compost as a fertilizer usually have little knowledge of what scientific compost really is.

It is what takes place in a growing plant from its first appearance above ground to blossoming time or thereabouts, that decides the plant's worth as compost material. While all plants require the same *basic* substances for their growth and development, plants differ widely in the materials which they gather directly from the soil. For instance, many plants send their roots far down into the lower soil regions and in this way collect specific ingredients which they need particularly. These special substances, often differing widely among plant groups, play a large part in giving compost its high value. As an example of this, field sorrel, though not an extensive forager, is an avid user of phosphorus and seems able to supply its wants completely, though a chemical analysis of the surface soil where it grows may reveal almost no phosphorus. There are many species of plants that are able to forage in the lower soils and thereby collect materials which the surface soils do not provide effectively. Some of these substances, naturally, are stored up in the plant bodies and go into the compost stack when the plants are cut and thus utilized. Therefore the quality of the compost is gauged, to a high degree, by the diversity of the plants which go into its making.

The wise compost builder gathers in these food-filled plants while they are still vigorous and green, thus building rich plant food from "greens," whereas Nature must wait until the life cycle has been completed. To this green richness is added other materials, consisting of barnyard manure and a definite portion of good soil which has mixed with it the very necessary lime for controlling excess acidity during the processing of the compost, and any other minerals or nitrates that may be desired. With this procedure, a far more complete and more naturally available fertilizer can be obtained than by any other means. No matter how valuable the manure or the sum total of the other ingredients that go in with the soil, the heart of good compost is what is found in the green vegetation, particularly when this consists of deep-rooted weeds.

The late Sir Albert Howard of England must be accorded the honor of being the father of modern, scientific compost. Sir Albert proved what could be done with his compost in bringing cultivated land to the highest point of productivity. As is ever the case with innovators, Sir Albert had to face the resistance of traditional thought. But he stuck by his guns and by the time of his passing a few years ago, compost built according to the Howard formula was recognized in many parts of the world as fertilizer with no equal. Just lately I received a communication from a region in South Africa which expressed surprise that American farmers had not yet accepted the Howard compost, or some substitute for it, as indispensable to quality food production. With farmers in that part of Africa the question no longer is whether or not to use the compost, but rather how to use it more effectively.

While I was working out my own problems of soil management in the Philippines, Sir Albert Howard was establishing his compost proofs in India. Sir Albert's tests were extremely varied, yet always practical. Every claim made for his compost was verified many times and under numerous conditions before the information was released. This English scientist cautioned persistently that halfhearted interest in compost farming could easily lead to disappointment. With Sir Albert composting was serious business because he felt strongly that it could meet a crying need in the world's agriculture. For this reason he did everything within his power to convince farmers and gardeners that compost making was far from child's work, as so many believed. He urged that composting be accepted as an important chore on the farm the same as other farm jobs, and then given a chance to prove its worth.

In order to do composting efficiently, Sir Albert advised that there be a special, permanent lot set apart on the farm for the compost yard. This permits the composting agents—the various groups of the soil microbes—to multiply in the area in enormous numbers. Composting is not possible without these valuable germs. Earthworms are also valuable workers in a compost stack as soon as the temperature, which is high in the initial period, drops to a condition suitable for their existence. And to assure easy access of the organisms to the compost stack, the latter should be started on clean, level ground, with nothing between the first compost layer and the soil.

The Howard stack may be built as long as desired, but a correct width is important. If too narrow the materials will dry out easily and bacterial action will thus be restricted, and if too wide the interior does not receive sufficient air for the germs. The recommended width is six or seven feet. The stack is built in layers, and wherever possible the first layer, the one spread over the ground, should be a *mixture* of green stuff six inches thick. Here is where we want that plant diversification already discussed. Since these green materials cannot be obtained during the winter in most sections, dry stuff can be used and the diversification rule applies here as with green materials. Weeds and crop leavings, either dry or green or mixed, forest leaves—all should find a place in this vegetation layer. I knew one enthusiastic compost builder who vied with himself to enlarge his diversification in each new compost stack. In time that called for considerable foraging on his part. His wife accused him of going so far as to pilfer her garden and carry off some of her choice vegetables and flowers.

The second layer of the Howard stack is made of fairly clean manure. Barnyard litter—bedding saturated with urine, etc.—should go into the stack also, but this should form a part of the vegetation layer. The solid manure may come from poultry, cattle, horses—from any livestock available. A mixture of manures is particularly good, and if fresh manures are used they should be permitted to dry out so as to make them easier to handle. It is via the manure layer that the compost maker puts into his stack huge numbers of virile microbes to strengthen those that come up from the ground. The manure also contains valuable nutrients, but the microbes are particularly important in helping to speed up the processing of the compost.

In building the third layer of the compost the tyro may go astray. This layer should be made of the best soil available. It is through the soil layer that the farmer, or gardener, puts into his compost the extra minerals or nitrates which he may think his soil needs. A sprinkling of agricultural lime must go into the stack with each soil layer, no matter what else may be omitted. As explained elsewhere, the lime is necessary for controlling the acids that develop during the disintegration of the organic substances. Many efficient compost builders like to add a bit of wood ashes and ground phosphate rock to strengthen the potash and phosphorus in the final produce. In case strong commercials are employed, as some prefer, these should be used in smaller quantities, say a fourth or a third as much as where the slow-actors are used. While I like best the slow-acting materials in my compost, the more active chemicals are satisfactory if the quantity is held to no more than a light sprinkling for each soil layer. This layer of soil in which the extra fertilizer ingredients are mixed should not be more than a fourth inch in thickness. If too thick it will form a sort of impervious layer and thus prevent proper air circulation throughout the stack. Since it is not an easy matter to state exactly what a *sprinkling* of materials means, if the compost builder will keep in mind that it is much easier to get too much material rather than too little when working with small quantities, and then operate accordingly, he is not likely to make a serious mistake.

From now on the procedure is repetition: six inches of vegetation, all possible kinds; a two-inch layer of barnyard manure, unless the manure is from poultry, where an inch is sufficient; the soil layer with its sprinkling of agricultural lime and any other minerals desired, including nitrates. As the stack goes up, both the vegetation layer and the manure layer should be thoroughly soaked immediately after being laid. Much more water will of course be required for the dry materials than for the green stuff, and weather conditions will also influence the amount of watering necessary. These are points that will have to be learned through practice.

The stack should be built to approximately five feet in height, layer upon layer, and should not be tamped more than what is absolutely necessary. Nature will do her own settling. On completion the stack is topped with hay, straw, or soil, and the top should be left concave so as to catch the rain, especially during the dry months of summer. Where long stacks are built, after placing the first layer, posts of a few inches in diameter should be stationed down the middle every three or four feet, then removed when the stack is finished. The holes will serve as ventilators.

Three weeks after the stack's completion it should be turned completely, the outside going to the center. Here is where many a would-be compost farmer turns back. He doesn't like this pitchfork phase. However, an ingenious farmer will devise a satisfactory method of turning his compost stacks. In sections where composting has become a real business, local brains have solved the turning problem. Five or six weeks after the first turning the stack is turned the second time, and a month later the compost is ready for use or for storage. Here is one solution:

Mr. Leonard Wickenden, biochemist, down-to-earth farmer, and compost authority, has evolved a compost formula that adheres fundamentally to the formula of Sir Albert Howard, yet which employs a few advantageous short-cuts. Instead of ricks, Wickenden builds round stacks six feet in diameter, and he turns his stacks but once, at the end of five weeks. Otherwise he follows closely the Howard formula: a six-inch layer of mixed vegetation; the manure layer; and the soil layer with its indispensable lime. Mr. Wickenden seems to prefer poultry manure, but he cautions care in the use of this due to its extra strength. He also holds the soil layer to no more than an eighth of an inch, or two ordinary shovels of earth for each soil layer in his six-foot stack. The lime must always go in with the soil, but, according to this authority, the lime is the only mineral needed for building perfect compost.

For small areas in town or elsewhere, there are good methods of making compost other than those just described. Where space is limited it is often desirable to compost in boxes. These boxes can be made from rough, one by six lumber, and it is usually good practice to run two boxes so as to have finished compost on hand whenever it is needed. One box, though, will produce a lot of rich fertilizer. A common size for these boxes is a length of about four feet, a width of two feet, and a height of four feet. Actually, the gardener's space and desires should govern the size of his compost boxes.

The boards on sides, ends, and bottom should be placed so as to leave cracks between them of a half inch or so, to provide for aeration. Some prefer bottomless boxes for a more free access of the soil organisms. On one side it will be advantageous to hinge the lower board to the one above, thus providing a door through which to secure compost while processing is going on in the upper part of the box.

As in the Howard and Wickenden composts, whenever possible the box compost should be started with a layer of green vegetation. Since the space is limited, the green stuff should be chopped and bruised before it is gently pressed into the box. Once there is a supply of compost on hand, some of this "live earth" should be mixed with the first layer and sprinkled into the other layers as pepping-up material. And that important rule still holds: the more diversified the ingredients that go into the box the better will be the compost. Weeds of all sorts and lawn mowings and fallen leaves are excellent for box composting.

The second layer so far as possible should be composed of kitchen garbage, and practically everything but tin cans and acids should find a place here: coffee grounds, scraps, vegetable left-overs, bones, chicken innards, etc. Here is a chance to transform such waste into the best of soil food for all sorts of gardening. It will result in the kind of fertilizer that will produce quality blossoms, enhancing both size and brilliance of color. In warm weather, this kind of compost may offend local sanitary regulations in town, but in the country the compost heap can be placed away from dwellings.

On top of the garbage there should be spread a thin layer of barnyard manure if such is available. All live-stock manures are excellent, including that from goats and rabbits. The compost will still be good fertilizer even if animal manures are not part of it, but with the manure the compost will be better. If the barnyard waste is used, this layer should be followed by a layer of good soil not much more than one-fourth inch thick. If there is no manure, the soil is spread over the garbage. The lime, as with the other composts, should go in with the soil, and when any quantity of dry leaves go into the box, a light sprinkling of some nitrate fertilizer will hasten the disintegration of the leaves.

This system of layering should be followed until the box is full. It is not necessary to fill the box completely at one time, so long as it is kept covered with a piece of canvas or something similar. Water, of course, should always be available for wetting the vegetation and garbage, and the manure, too, if the latter is used, when they are first put into the box. When full the box should be topped with a layer of soil fairly thick. This soil blanket will tend to give an earthy effect to all that lies below. It is also advisable to have a covering of fine-mesh wire to keep out pilfering animals.

Yes, we agree—emphatically! The composting methods described thus far are especially adapted to intensive farming and gardening. Neither belongs in extensive land management in the United States, because of the labor problem, and too often because of a shortage of composting materials. However, the latter is not so much of a limiting factor as many would have it. In Europe and Africa and Asia, where cheap labor is more abundant, the Howard compost long ago proved its adaptability to large estates of all kinds.

This impracticability of compost-stack farming on our large, machine-run farms in this country does not in the least make less valuable the compost in efficient agriculture. Compost will improve the land to the point where the produce harvested from that land is uniformly *quality* produce. And no one can deny that we need to improve the quality of food taken from our large farms as much as we need to improve that harvested from gardens. This is the necessity which has given rise to *sheet-*

composting. Sheet composting is the Howard compost adapted to large-scale farming under American conditions.

The first step in sheet-composting is to make sure that the mineral content of the land to be composted is strong. Lime, however, should not be applied as a rule beyond a ton per acre. The reason for this will be discussed later. In starting out, some phosphate will be needed, and if rock phosphate is used, it should be applied at the rate of about two hundred pounds per acre. Should superphosphate be employed instead of the rock, the super should be held to not more than seventy-five to one hundred pounds per acre. On very poor land a *light application* of some commercial nitrate may possibly be advisable also. The slow-acting minerals appear to be a bit more trustworthy in sheet-composting, but the quick-actors will work satisfactorily if they are used sparingly, at least until the soil has a fairly good sponge. The organic content of the land is likely to be low when one starts out to improve it via the sheet-compost method, so don't run the risk of burning up the few biological agents that are going to be needed more than anything else in reviving the soil's workshop.

The second step in sheet-composting is to grow on the land which has previously received its mineral applications and probably some nitrates, a diversified *green manure.* This should be a mixture with legumes predominating. The ideal crop for sheet-composting is a mixture of two or three legumes, at least one cereal like oats or rye, and whatever weeds move in. We must not forget that this green crop is the vegetation layer of the compost stack. A thin planting of each of several crops normally is better than a thick planting of a single crop, though sheet-composting can be done very well with only one green crop. All members of this combined planting must be seasonable, naturally.

While the "vegetation layer" is making its growth, the problem of the manure for the indispensable manure layer can receive attention. There can be no complete sheet-composting without this manure layer any more than compost stacks can be built without it. Just as in the stack, the manure should be on the ground during the processing period of the green stuff. This will usually mean that it is to be scattered directly onto the vegetation at the rate of five or six tons per acre only a short time before the crop is to be disked thoroughly and turned under, which is some time around the blossoming period of the legumes. The manure, if not too fresh, will carry into the soil not only a vigorous collection of beneficial microbes, but some of the valuable molds which always go along with highly productive land. If the manure is not spread over the growing vegetation, it should be spread immediately the green crop has gone down.

Unfortunately, there are some drawbacks to composting in the field. The various ingredients will not "compost" unless the moisture and temperature are right. These factors in a correctly built stack are largely under control, but, save in irrigated fields, not otherwise. Where there is ample moisture and the temperature correct for strong bacterial action, the same processing goes on in the field as in the stack, only at a slower pace. It takes six or more months to complete the field processing, and during this time the land should not be disturbed. Which is to say that a farmer with a large acreage should arrange to compost only a reasonable part of his land each season. Any claim that such procedure is not feasible is not based on sound logic. A dangerously high percentage of our American soils are in dire need of this natural soil treatment. Surely taking a field out of production for a year in order to start it on the comeback road is sensible land management, even though every acre may be needed for immediate crops. There might be some immediate loss, but in the long run there would be real gain.

Sheet-composting is a refreshing trend back to Nature and her sensible ways. The sheet-compost is much like Nature's vegetative mulch, so when man does a good job at sheet-composting, Nature smiles.

The extent to which sheet-composting can be practiced will depend upon the amount of barnyard manure available. And since even one ordinary milch cow will produce from thirteen to fifteen tons of manure per year (solid and liquid combined), and since five tons of manure are ample for sheet-composting an acre once, the common excuse of non-available manure largely vanishes. Horses produce only slightly less manure per thousand-pound weight than do cattle, and even a hundred hens will surprise one with the quantity of high-quality manure they turn off. A thousand pounds of poultry will deliver around six tons of *concentrated* manure annually. If one counts only the period that cows are corraled, he will still be able to salvage seven or eight tons of manure per animal, and every acre strengthened through sheet-composting is an acre of quality soil added to the farm.

There is one other type of compost that gives promise of ultimately replacing the compost stack entirely. That is, it will probably replace the compost stack as soon as machines for grinding up the materials become more common. Here the various materials are run through a shredder or grinder, in about the same proportion they are layered in the stack. The stuff comes from the machine much as straw from a thresher. In case the machine does not do a thorough job of mixing, this can be taken care of with a few turns of the pitchfork. Nothing more is needed except to see that the stack is moistened properly as it goes up. Nature will do the rest and do it in a remarkably short time. For best results in machine composting, it seems essential to inoculate the shredded materials with a compost "starter." More will be said about compost starters later on.

Through the use of a grinder I have been able to produce usable compost within a period of three weeks. For the "soil layer" I like to use old compost made from a large assortment of weeds and other materials, including several kinds of tree leaves. This "live earth" serves as a very efficient starter. Since at the present time we do not know with absolute certainty which weeds contain the special activating substances, it is wise to employ as large an assortment as possible. My own results verify this.

Doctor Ehrenfried Pfeiffer in his Bio-Dynamic laboratory at Spring Valley, New York, has probably given closer study to scientific compost starters of several kinds than any other scientist in America. This biochemist defines his basic starter as follows: "A selected and carefully prepared group of humus-fixing bacteria carried on a natural medium enriched with growth hormones and enzymes."

In other words, Dr. Pfeiffer's activators, or compost starters, consist of active bacteria supported by enzymes and hormones. Hormones and enzymes are substances which stimulate the life processes of both plants and animals. All plants contain these substances to a degree, but some plants are richer in them than others. These special weeds, already discussed, are the ones that carry the materials abundantly into the compost. With the compost thus thoroughly inoculated, both by means of the special weeds and the prepared starter, the processing is speeded up so that one can have usable compost in a fraction of the time possible with the old methods. However, the starters can be used with excellent success in all of the composts described, even in sheet-composting. In a future chapter the marvelous work now being done by Dr. Pfeiffer with his "pedigreed microbes" will be discussed more completely.

And now the finale on compost farming—composting those fallen leaves which are always so unwelcome in the fall! To begin with, if you own a tree in town, don't burn the leaves! To burn this rich source of natural minerals is tragic, particularly since the processing of the leaves is so simple.

One good method of composting leaves is to mix them

with weeds and then layer the mixture into small stacks with alternating layers of barnyard manure. If manure is not available, then just stack the weed-leaf mixture in an out-of-the-way place, soaking the materials well with water as the stack goes up. And if there are no weeds, just pile up the leaves with lawn mowings, or alone, and let Nature do the rest. But don't destroy this valuable plant food!

Some like to sprinkle the leaves with a nitrate fertilizer in solution as they build the stack, claiming this helps to break down the stubborn leaf tissues, all of which is true. But about the same results can be obtained with barnyard manure. The important thing is to compost the fallen leaves and with this excellent fertilizer improve those weak spots in the lawn, perk up the hungry roses and other shrubbery, or use the compost in growing a few choice vegetables and flowers. In autumn leaves are golden; in value they are gold.

3

Green Manures

GREEN MANURE farming is of ancient origin. Old Roman agricultural literature urges the use of green materials for building up and maintaining soil fertility, especially when lentils (a kind of pea) and medic (the ancestor of our present alfalfa) were employed as the land-improving crops. But it was the Chinese who long have depended upon green manures as an almost indispensable source of natural fertilizer. It is entirely probable that China could not have survived as she has for so many centuries had it not been for her farmers' persistent use of greens in their heavily cropped soils. During my soil survey of South China, all the better-class farmers were strong in their insistence that nothing could take the place of "green compost." Their green compost is merely green vegetation chopped up and added to the soil directly. Cultivated land, I was informed on every hand, would not give its highest production without this green stuff worked into it from time to time, no matter how much night soil or other fertilizing materials might be applied. The green compost has been prized so highly and for so long by the Chinese farmers that the rocky hills have become almost denuded to obtain vegetation for making it.

With most farmers in the United States and in most parts of Europe, green-manuring is largely a hit-and-miss proposition. Farmers, as a rule, do not have a clear concept as to just what advantages may accrue to them from turning green crops into their soils. Actually, there are three major gains to be derived from green-manure farming, and which of these three is most important in a particular soil problem will depend upon the soil to be treated. To illustrate, on extremely poor land the most urgent need is likely to be the replacement of the sponge structure of the soil, irrespective of whether the soil is sand or clay. Such land always needs nutrients, too, but to pour fertilizer into land that does not contain at least some organic substances for absorbing and holding the fertilizing materials, is largely waste. In sandy soils where there is no sponge to bind the particles of sand together, the applied ingredients trickle straight through, and in clays the opposite condition is likely to exist. That is, the soil particles are pushed together so completely there is little chance for the fertilizing substances to penetrate the soil.

With such land—and that kind of land is very common where erosion is rampant—the farmer's job is to establish in it some sponge structure as quickly as he can get it done, to fiberize it. Anything that can be induced to grow and produce sponge-making material should be looked upon with favor. After a working sponge has been established, then will be the time to think about a more select green manure for strengthening the nutrients in the soil. During this initial stage, though—sage brush or noxious weeds; choice legumes or the best of cereals—a farmer shouldn't frown upon anything that will help him put back into the land its original fibrous condition.

In working towards the improvement of land that is already reasonably productive, the story is quite different. While even that soil is certain to need some improvement in its sponge structure, along with this build-up of the sponge there will also be need of *enriching* the land. Or, putting it another way, the chief aim is likely to be to strengthen the weak links of the fertility chain, though the farmer is probably not thinking of it that way. Not being interested in compost of any kind, it is quite probable that the farmer expects to get from his green manures the greater portion of the soil-improving materials which he believes his soil needs. Owing to this special demand which he is going to make upon his green manures, he will need to be more selective in choosing his green-manure crops. In other words, he is going to choose, grow, and work into his soil the crops that will do this exacting job for him in the most efficient manner possible. And if he follows present farming practices, his green manure will be legumes. Today in our country, green manures and legumes are almost synonymous terms.

The discovery by a Dutch scientist during the latter part of the last century that nitrogen-fixing bacteria make their homes in knots or nodules on the roots of pod-bearing plants, is largely responsible for the universal belief that legumes are the only plants that improve the soil. The

Dutchman's discovery crowned the legume as monarch among soil greens, for nitrogen in both Europe and America, even at that period, was looked upon as a common limiting factor in crop production.

It is an interesting secret—shall we say—of Nature that, though three-fourths of the air we breathe consists of nitrogen gas, plants are unable to use this gas for making food in their leaves until certain soil microbes work the nitrogen over. As a rule, though, farmers and many scientists, too, since the Dutchman's discovery, have been giving the legumes, along with their nodules containing the nitrogen-fixers, more credit than the legumes have had coming to them. Usually farmers think mostly of the available nitrogen that a green-manure will put into their soils, whereas nitrogen is but *one* value to be derived from green-manure farming.

The fact of the matter is, legumes are not always the best crops for feeding a soil its greens, despite the extra nitrogen they are supposed to supply the soil. Marcus Cato the Roman agriculturist who gave lessons in farm management centuries ago, lists some legumes that were injurious to the land and cautioned farmers not to use them in their composts or in their crop rotations. Farmers of today know that legumes differ widely in their effects on the soil. Actually, many members of the grass family —rye for example—will do a better job of improving land than will most of the pod-bearers, especially when a quick build-up is desired in the top layer of soil.

A German scientist by the name of Peklo seems to have been the first to discover the presence of nitrogen-fixing organisms *inside* the roots of non-leguminous plants. Peklo's discovery is mentioned in the German edition of Professor Molisch's *Plant Physiology*, published in 1920. Until this discovery, it was not clear why cereal crops were particularly good green-manures. With such a vast number of fibrous roots working so close to the surface of the soil, and with these roots containing nitrogen-fixers, the fertilizing power of rye, for instance, is certain to be very considerable. By utilizing this fixed nitrogen to build protein, and with this protein temporarily stored in the young rye before the latter is turned under, it is not difficult to see how valuable the cereals can be in improving the soils in orchards, gardens, etc. Wheat, barley, and oats would probably serve equally well as green manures. Naturally, many will disagree with Peklo's concept of nitrogen-fixing bacteria living and working inside the roots of cereals. Even so, the fact still remains that young cereals make excellent green manures.

And green-manuring with several varieties of weeds will often improve the soil more than will either the legumes or the grasses. If a farmer wishes to give some particular field a special treatment, after making sure the field is fairly strong in lime and phosphate, let him apply a hundred pounds or so of some commercial nitrate fertilizer per acre, and then turn this land to weeds for a season. The weeds will gobble up the nitrates along with whatever other nutrients are available, and then with their highly nourished root-systems they will explore the lower soils and pump back to the surface of the soil not only more minerals, but other nutrients, including some of the most valuable trace elements. This means that the bodies of the weeds will be heavy with valuable materials while they are lush and green, and should be disked down when in that stage of growth and worked into the soil. Just as with weeds in the compost, the more diversified the weed crop, the more richness it will put into the soil. When these weeds decay they return to the surface soil much more than they took out of it, and material in a highly nutritious form. This isn't saying that a farmer is going to turn his farm over to weeds. But rare is the farm that does not have at least some land that can be amazingly helped by means of this weed treatment. For purifying land that has become infested for one reason or another, nothing can surpass a dose of well-fed weeds.

Dr. Anna Koffler of Kansas City, Missouri, an authority on microbes of the soil, has found that the soil surrounding the roots of healthy weeds is teeming with active beneficial microbes—a very good guarantee that the weeds improve the soil's fertility, especially when the weeds are worked back into the soil while green, as I have suggested. Even when growing thinly, as companions of other crops, many weeds are constructive workers. Though Dr. Koffler's investigations have dealt largely with pigweeds, lamb's quarter, and a few other old familiars, she assures us there is no apparent reason to believe the same condition does not obtain with a large number of other common weeds. Probably not all weeds are thus beneficial, but the point is that many weeds are assets when correctly put to work.

The soil that Nature requires for best plant growth is a complicated workshop—this fundamental fact needs constant repetition. In this workshop there are many active agents whose task it is to process materials for use by the plant for growth and development. According to Nature's universal laws, while these various agents are working for themselves, as shown by the microbes that flourish around many weed roots, they are also laboring for the plant and through the plant for the rest of us. We can no more exist without the fruits of their labors than we can exist without air. That is why the farmer's chief soil-management task is to see that conditions are right in his land for his microbes. And these germs, along with the beneficial molds and the earthworms, are ravenous eaters. Most of them feed upon organic materials, and all must likewise have their minerals, either fed to them by the farmer in the form of a commercial product, or brought up from the subsoil by deep-foraging weeds and through earthworm circulation.

Scientists have known these facts for a long time, but not so long has it been recognized that the microbes also require their *special* greens. This is the third value to be derived from green manures. It is now believed that chlorophyll, or some other substance in the leaves with which the chlorophyll is associated, may even be the most valuable substance which the microbes themselves derive from green manures. The microbes can get their protein, of which nitrogen is the vital element, from sources other than the green crop. There are several groups of germs, some of which are even more important nitrogen fixers than those that live in nodules, but in cultivated land there is likely to be a deficiency of the greens which the microbes seem to demand, and it is up to the farmer to supply these greens as nearly as possible as the microbes demand them.

In naturally fertile land that is not under cultivation, or in good pasture areas where a healthy sponge has been constructed from grass roots, there is an abundance of tiny green plants which botanists call algae. These algae grow and multiply in the first six or eight inches of such soils, and, one has reason to conclude, keep the microbes well supplied with all the greens they need. In land under continuous cultivation it is another matter, because the algae are constantly disturbed and even destroyed in large numbers. So if the microbes in such soils are to get their greens, the farmer will have to provide them by means of green manures.

And there is a right way and right age for putting these special greens into the soil for the microbes. Biochemists who have worked on this problem extensively have discovered that plants contain a higher amount of *quality* food, especially protein, and in all likelihood foods that are particularly acceptable to the soil germs, just as the plant starts to prepare for flower development. According to Dr. C. F. Schnobel, a biochemist of Kansas City who has spent a large part of his life studying the food value of grasses, the high food stage in the latter crops occurs when jointing starts and for a short period thereafter. In other plants this high food period occurs a short time before they start putting out buds.

Letting the green crop grow until it has made all the growth possible will of course, benefit the land enormously. This is particularly true of green manures, which, when worked into the soil after they have reached an advanced stage of growth, add a far greater quantity of fiber, which is essential in building the soil's sponge, than will the young manures. Also, the old crop will contain a greater assortment of nutrients than have been collected in the lower soils, a fact which must always be taken into consideration when farming with green manures. But for greens to feed the microbes, the processors of practically all food substances which go into solution in the soil, the young green manures are best.

The Chinese are aware of this importance of working young green vegetation into their land that is intensively cultivated. They look upon this as a vital part of their soil-management program. One of their green-manure practices is to grow soy beans with their other crops, then, when these soys are three or four inches high, to pull the soys and force them back into the soil, roots up. Almost invariably when I talked with Chinese farmers, they would explain that this practice produced not only a quicker crop but a larger crop than when the young greens were omitted. Composting and other methods of land fertilization were also essential, however. As the Chinese saw this use of young greens, it was a necessity in holding their land to the highest possible production level.

The question naturally arises, will young green manure, when turned under, supply the same quality of greens to the following crop as when the greens are grown with the major crop? While more research needs to be done before a complete answer can be given to this question, it is possible that the Chinese system is more nearly the ideal. And on small, intensive areas this would usually be possible, but not with non-row crops nor in extensive farming. On the other hand, when a separate green manure is grown for the purpose of feeding a soil its greens, the subsequent crop will surely benefit—*for it is the soil microbes we are going to feed directly and the following crop only indirectly.* By the time the major crop does come along, so long as the interval is reasonably short, the microbes themselves will be better fed and naturally better prepared to nourish the latter crop. So in farming with green manures, the farmer will need to keep always in mind those three basic values: to build a soil sponge; to pump plant nutrients up from the deeper soils and add these to the surface soil through the decay of the plants; and to provide greens for the microbes specifically, in order to equip them to do more efficient work. As the microbes die, the nourishment from their decayed bodies also reaches the plant.

But merely growing a green manure and turning it under haphazardly is far from being all there is to green-manuring. To get the most out of a green manure, like anything else on the farm, it should receive the right kind of treatment. Farmers who are not sympathetic towards compost farming of any kind, and for those who refuse to recognize any kind of green manures except legumes— then legumes it should be for all they are worth. Inoculated legumes combined with a fair growth—not a thick growth—of some of our choice weeds like sunflower, rag-weeds, lamb's quarter, etc., will make a green manure hard to beat. The soil in all types of green-manure farming should be kept reasonably supplied with agricultural lime, because legumes call for a bit more calcium than do most other crops. Lime will also be needed to control the organic acids that arise from the decay of such an abundance of vegetation. A weed-legume combination with lime where needed, and two hundred pounds per acre of rock phosphate—or seventy-five to one hundred pounds of super in case this phosphate is desired—this system of land management followed persistently will in time do wonders to depleted soil.

Some knowledge of the soil's agricultural history is always helpful in rebuilding the fertility chain in land, no matter what system of land improvement is employed. For satisfying success with the green-manure method, two procedures are basic: a continuous use of the green crops as a part of the rotation, and a shifting of varieties so as to put different types of root systems to work in the soil to as great an extent as can be done feasibly. When a farmer is ready to cast aside superstition and employ those *good* weeds that are available to him no matter where, employing them along with his legumes, he will not only do a better job of green manuring, but he will complete the job in shorter than the usual time. *Diversification is fundamental!* Three different legumes, or legumes mixed with cereal crops, is far better than a single thick crop. One of these different crops should be a shallow feeder, one a deep feeder, and one should work mostly in the intermediate soil zone. Farmers will generally find that they have at their disposal crops ample to meet these requirements.

The actual growing of a green manure is not as important as the right inculcation of the crop into the soil. If one is a "mulch farmer," he will still need to turn under a crop now and then so as to maintain the sponge in the deeper soils. Vigorous roots will go far towards keeping up this sponge in the upper layer of subsoil, but they will not take care of it farther down, especially in land under continuous cultivation. Those who do not approve of the surface mulch should plan to turn their green manures under at different depths. From time to time a crop should be forced down as deeply as implements and available motive power will put it. Also there should be intermediate turnings now and then, in addition to working the green stuff into the shallow surface. Variation again!

The Chinese system of bruising the materials before working them into the soil is definitely scientific. Tearing up and multilating the green vegetation starts fermentation above ground, and this permits quicker disintegration within the soil. Even during early spring and late fall, when the temperature does not permit quick wilting, it is good business to disk the green crop well before turning, and double-disk immediately afterwards. The microbes in the soil will then be able to accomplish enough more to compensate the farmer for all the extra labor he gives to the breaking down of the crop. As stated elsewhere, bacteria and molds and earthworms can get down to the basic business of processing the final products without having to spend so much time in roughage.

In bringing back "lost land," or even ordinarily poor land, getting that first green crop well on its way may prove difficult. Here perhaps more than anywhere else in working to improve land, patience and persistence will be needed. The chances are that the land has become sick only after many years of maltreatment. To give such land a shot in the arm with a light application of some good commercial may be advisable at the outset. Even the most hardy weeds will appreciate this. The important thing is not to overdo with the commercials while the soil contains no sponge—the old reminder again. Very poor land may require three or four years of unremitting natural treatment before there is any noticeable response. It is always helpful, though, when attacking difficult soil problems, to remember: *Nature does not accept defeat.* A sick field, no matter where it is, can be healed unless conditions there obtain that absolutely prevent the operation of Nature's constructive methods.

On denuded land, the farmer will have to give serious thought to how much soil-stirring he is going to do before he plants that first crop. Too much tillage rather than too little can easily be the worst procedure. Since this first crop is likely to be meager at best, uncovered loose soil, if on any kind of slope, will mean further erosion. But every plant that makes it through, be that plant rye or legume or annual weed, and sends its roots down to a fair depth—that plant should be looked upon as being truly constructive. After the first crop the green-manures will gradually grow better, and every weed that offers to join in the fray should be welcomed.

Vegetable and flower gardeners usually overlook the benefits possible from green-manuring their soils. Even compost gardeners or mulch gardeners should employ green manures in a systematic rotation. That custom of the Chinese of growing a thick crop of soy beans with their garden crops, is excellent gardening and will work equally well elsewhere, whether it is in a vegetable garden or a choice flower garden. Cowpeas or garden beans, or field or garden peas, or even rye or oats, depending on the time of year the gardener may wish to use them, will work as well as soys. Broadcasting the legumes, or cereals, among the vegetables and flowers, and then working the young plants in as a surface mulch with the hoe when they are a few inches tall, may be playing Oriental but it will pay high dividends if followed year after year.

Where space allows, strip gardening is an excellent way of growing superior vegetables and superb flowers, and maintaining a strong fertility chain at the same time. This can be done through a system of green-manure rotation. Narrow strips of vegetables or flowers can be alternated with narrow strips of legumes, the legume strips treated very lightly with agricultural lime. The vegetables and flowers should change places with the legumes season after season. After the legumes have completed most of their growth but are still tender and full of life, the gardener has the choice of chopping them up and turning the green stuff under, or employing it as compost material and then returning the finished compost to the soil.

Either method is good, and where both are used, that is, where every other legume strip goes under and where the others are given to the compost, even more good will result. That is gardening with Nature and it is good gardening.

Green manures alone are not a complete fertilizer, but if the diversification suggested in this chapter is followed, a very satisfactory fertility chain can be established and maintained in any normal soil. This method of farming will not bring forth a perfect soil, but it will produce a good soil. I suspect that few gardeners realize that the vigorous young weeds that come up so healthy in their gardens—those annoying pests—are natural fertilizers. They haven't gathered up quantities of minerals in the lower soils, but most of them have accumulated quality nutrients even at that young age. Unless these youngsters are clearly causing specific trouble, it is wise to let them grow up a few inches, chop them into shreds with the hoe, and then work that material into the surface of the soil. This can be done without permitting the weed growth to smother the vegetables or flowers if the latter are planted in rows. The good results thus obtained will not be as conspicuous as the *deceptive* results that at times are obtained through the use of stimulating products, but the former will be decidedly more constructive.

4

Soil Minerals, Commercials

OF every morsel of *real* food consumed by plants and animals, 96 per cent is built from the four food elements, carbon, hydrogen, oxygen, and nitrogen. These are the same chemical elements we inhale when we breathe; they make up practically all of the atmosphere. That leaves less than 4 per cent of all our food materials to come *directly* from the soil. Just 4 per cent—yet how mighty is that 4 per cent in sustaining life on the earth!

Without going too much into technicalities, we can safely say that it is this mighty 4 per cent which gives us our "mineral foods": our accessory foods, as they are sometimes called. Though seemingly needed in very small quantities, these minerals are just as essential to growth and other life processes as are foods made from the comparatively greater volume of materials derived from the air. These mineral indispensables are generally known to most of us: phosphorus or phosphate, sulfur, potassium or potash, calcium or lime, and magnesium. The members of this group are the five majors. With the possible exception of phosphate, lime, and potash, usually when we hear any of these elements mentioned we do not think of them as plant and animal food substances, yet plants will not grow at all when any one of them is completely lacking in the soil. And there are still other soil elements which are probably equally important. These latter are often called the minors or trace elements, because they are needed in such minute quantities. There is a very large number of these so-called minors, but the ones which at the present time are believed to be absolutely essential are iron, boron, copper, zinc, and manganese. We are almost daily learning more about the trace elements, and while our knowledge as to their exact place in plant and animal growth is still very incomplete, it is quite probable that more than those listed may be found to be essentials. These and other food minerals will be discussed further in a later chapter.

In any consideration of soil minerals, it is helpful to keep in mind the difference between food and food substances. Food is the finished product turned out through photosynthesis in the leaves of plants, or formed by enzymes elsewhere in the plant; whereas the food substances are the ingredients from which the original foods are made. Just how the materials taken in directly from the soil, and the air nutrients which reach the plant through the soil, get into the feeder roots is still mostly theory. Scientists are not in agreement as to how it is done. The latest thought is that the rootlets themselves do not actually come in contact with the food substances. This is because the feeder roots are covered with certain types of microbes, and it is these germs which take up the nutrients which are in solution in the soil water, and then pass these on into the roots after giving them a working-over. Then the materials are sent on their way, up to the leaves or elsewhere in the plant where they are needed. These bacteria or germs covering the feeder roots are a species of middlemen who not only stand guard over what shall or shall not enter the plant, but by the processing which they give the nutrients possibly refine them in some way we don't yet understand. And while some materials always get into the plant that apparently do not belong there, on the whole the germs would appear to be pretty efficient policemen as well as middlemen.

All of which brings us to the two controversial terms, "organic" and "inorganic" minerals, when applied to plant-food materials. Some scientists insist there is no difference between organic and inorganic minerals, saying that a mineral by its very nature is inorganic—it just is. And they are correct from the standpoint of technical chemistry. Sulfur is always sulfur and phosphorus is always phosphorus. Nevertheless, from the standpoint of agriculture it is permissible to talk about both organic and inorganic compounds when referring to food minerals. And therein lies the difference between "organic" minerals and "inorganic" minerals. These different compounds may not act at all alike when they are in the soil. The difference between organic and inorganic minerals can be seen in the work of trees. Tree roots, though they take up organic compounds in the upper layer of soils, in their foraging far and wide through the deeper soils the roots gather up dissolved mineral compounds where no plant or animal substances have entered into their formation. These inorganic compounds come generally from the original parent rocks, and in order to be assimilated must usually be in solution. After they have been processed in the tree leaves, new compounds result which contain the element carbon. The inclusion of this element makes the compound organic. When the leaves fall in the autumn, much of this mineral organic substance which was built up in the green leaves during the summer goes back to the soil, to be used again in the growth cycle. True, when these organic compounds are broken down, sulfur will be just sulfur again and phosphorus just phosphorus.

A brilliant analysis of plant nutrition is contained in Frank A. Gilbert's book, *Mineral Nutrition of Plants and Animals* (Norman, University of Oklahoma Press, 1948). William A. Albrecht of the University of Missouri is responsible for some of the most fruitful investigations in plant nutrition and the ultimate bearing of such nutrition upon animal and human health. Readers who may wish to pursue this field in its technical details will be well advised to consult the works of both of these writers.

Chemists can of course build compounds that carry the vital minerals much as Nature requires them. And chemists can likewise construct compounds so strong they completely upset the normal activities in the workshop of the soil, unless they are used with extreme caution. When man-made fertilizers are applied to the soil in a form that does not harmonize very closely with natural requirements, as the latter operate in the soil, several undesirable things *can* happen: plants may be stimulated into unnatural growth; or disturbances may be caused which interfere with the work of the biological agents that are chiefly responsible for the soil's permanent fertility. Then there are some commercial products which release substances that will, when in solution, get by the guards on the feeder roots and give the vegetation a disagreeable taste not relished by livestock. Many farmers are familiar with pastures where the animals dislike to eat the grass because of this.

When a farmer applies chemicals to his soils, he should keep always in mind the rule that will render such chemicals comparatively safe: a strong organic buffer. In pastures it is not so easy to take care of this as it is in cultivated fields, but even there much can be done by applying the stronger more sparingly and where there is a surface sponge. That is, where the grass has not been burned over.

Virgin forest soil, if free from erosion, practically always has a high mineral content and in an available form. This mineral richness is derived mostly from the continuous decay of the leaf carpet. These organically-held minerals, when the leaves first fall, are tightly held in the leaf tissues, and considerable time or special treatment may be required before they are released. In case one wishes to raid this mineral supply, the most practical manner of securing the minerals is to run the leaves through a compost. The owner of a large ranch in the Middle West, having learned about the valuable mineral content of leaves, contracted for the entire leaf output of a large city. That is, he agreed to haul the leaves away if the townspeople would pile them up for him. He is now composting these leaves for their sponge-forming qualities and their minerals. This farmer has vision.

Forest soils, like desert soils, have peculiar characteristics of their own which are not generally recognized. Those who are familiar with forest land brought under cultivation remember vividly the enormous crops they took from these lands the first two or three years; harvests always surpassing those from their best prairie lands. But these farmers are also likely to recall that these wonderfully rich soils showed signs of soil-depletion the third or fourth year after breaking, and not a great while thereafter were about the worst soils on the farm.

The quick depletion of forest land turned to cultivation appears to be traceable to two definite causes: while the surface layer of such land is extremely fertile at the outset, especially in organic mineral compounds, most of the nutrients in this "leaf mold" are immediately available owing to the strong activity of the molds and microbes. There is very little reserve save what is found in the undecayed leaf carpet. When the land is first broken, due to the fact that practically all food-nutrients are in solution, crops are able to gorge themselves like hogs breaking into a corncrib. And like the crib the soil soon contains little nourishment for oncoming crops.

Also, Nature's blueprint is not complete, in a forest, as a rule. The mulch is there to provide a sponge for the thin layer of top soil, but the land-improving weeds are not on the job with their fiberizing roots. The earthworms are at their tasks all right, but the worms, though they do bore into the lower soils to some extent and carry a few organic particles down there, in the forest earthworms are largely surface soil inhabitants, since they seem able to obtain all their needed minerals from the decayed leaves.

Therefore, subsoils are comparatively weak except in certain minerals. And any farm boy who has grown to manhood in a forest region can tell you how unsatisfactory farming is on old forest land. He remembers those fields as being spotted, with most of the spots extremely sick. Of all poor land on any farm, the once forest fields, if they have not received exceptionally constructive treatment all along, are the poorest and most difficult to bring back to life. The wild man of the jungles will tell you there is nothing to be done with such land except to move humans off it and return it to the gods for one lifetime.

Nevertheless, old forest land can be brought back to fertility, but the person who starts out to do it must make up his mind to do a lot of co-operating with Nature, and especially with her efficient weeds. Once land like this is brought back to life, its fertility is not difficult to maintain and it can be made to produce with the best. But by then it is no longer forest land of any kind—it is land completely reborn.

Many weeds will collect minerals as well as other nutrients in the lower soils and send these up to their leaves where they are transformed. It is this ability of some weeds to gather up and work over the inorganics found in the deeper soils which makes them such excellent green manures, not only for rebuilding old forest land, but for rebuilding most land. Therefore, when a mineral problem arises, a farmer's thoughts should first go straight to his subsoil—and to the weeds that are ready to help him. If his subsoil is normal, it probably contains both organic and inorganic mineral compounds, and enough to meet all his ordinary requirements. By striving to utilize these natural minerals along with his commercial products, a farmer will serve both his surface soil and his pocketbook.

In the heavier soils like the clays there are sticky materials called colloids which have a tendency to prevent the downward movement of the organic compounds into the subsoil, thus holding these organic materials largely near the surface. However, normal subsoils are known to contain both organic and inorganic compounds in comparative abundance, and, according to some biochemists, this is due to the fact that organic acids, the products of organic decay in the surface soil, move down into the subsoil and play an important part in developing new organic compounds down there. Not only will deep-rooted weeds and certain deep-rooted crops salvage a great deal of this subsoil material, but the roots of such crops when they die and decay in their tunnels, distribute minerals all through the soil. And one has only to do a bit of exploring with the shovel to discover what wonderful distributors earthworms are if the worms have an organically rich soil from which to operate.

Dr. Ehrenfried Pfeiffer, mentioned in an earlier chapter, has found that there is a continuous mineral circulation between the upper and lower soils where the soils are naturally strong. This mineral circulation is apparently necessary for a perfect functioning soil workshop. When the fertility chain is unbroken and all links are dynamically at work, this mineral circulation goes on harmoniously; just as harmoniously as the transpiration stream moves up a healthy plant. But let something come along to disturb this chain and there will most likely be deceptive signs of mineral deficiency. In the majority of such cases it is not an extra dose of minerals which the soil needs, but rather *an organic adjustment*. Repair the organics, get earthworms to work, and the trouble will usually vanish.

At this point Nature will, of course, move in with soil-improving weeds, and in some cases with short grasses, and straighten things out if the land is not further disturbed. Seldom, though, is Nature given a chance even to assist in solving the problem. With most people, the word *weed* spawns distrust like the word *snake*. Few are willing to accept the sane logic that many so-called weeds can be assets. Dr. Pfeiffer, through his extensive research on his own farms, has established conclusive evidence, evidence which is also substantiated in many other parts of the world, that there are weeds that collect and pump back to the surface specific minerals gathered below the reach of ordinary crops. There are many weeds that are able to collect minerals from a "higher dilution" in the surface soil than is possible with most domestic crops. These particular weeds, though chemical analysis shows the soil to be weak in a certain mineral, will contain in their tissues an abundance, more or less, of that mineral. No more proof than this is needed to show how clearly the mineral supply in the upper layers of soil is related to the work of beneficial weeds.

There are regions where cacti abound, and wherever this is the case these plants should be utilized through some form of compost for the minerals they accumulate. Growing cacti specifically for fertilizer could be a paying business, because these plants need not compete with other crops. Yarrow, a common pasture weed in many parts of the country, is a meticulous collector of both lime and potash. This fern-like weed has not a single obnoxious trait and should be gathered or even grown for the compost. Wild onions and garlic are excellent compost material because they are sulfur-gatherers. Where native, these plants will grow on stony areas and may well be encouraged. No doubt there are many other mineral-gatherers among local weeds in all parts of the United States. Some of these will resist domestication while others can be made to grow without too much trouble. On the whole, growing weeds successfully will be found to be an art that has to be learned. But the day is not far distant when such knowledge will be essential to good farming and gardening.

It is *mineral quality* rather than quantity that is vital in maintaining a strong fertility chain—notwithstanding the opposite claim of many soil scientists. Is it illogical to conclude that Nature has at hand, in most situations, the means for building up and maintaining a sufficiency of quality minerals? Few question Nature's methods of maintaining her nitrogen supply. And nitrogen, though not a mineral, is not only required in great abundance, but is difficult to keep under control—much more so than the minerals. Nature never does things by halves. Whatever the requirements for growth and the support of life, she provides these materials in sufficient amounts for normal purposes. This is not intended to say that mineral fertilizers are never to be applied to the soil. With the heavy demands that are levied upon our food producing lands, such applications are constantly necessary. The point is that the natural methods of obtaining the minerals should be recognized and utilized wherever possible, and to their fullest extent, with the commercials being employed as supplements only.

There is lack of sound reasoning on both sides of this "commercial fertilizer" question. The insistence by some groups that *all* chemicals are injurious to soil, to the plants grown on that soil, and ultimately to the humans who consume the foods thus produced, in *all* situations, is not based on realism. It just isn't true. But the opposite claim that *no* commercial fertilizers ever cause trouble in the soil's workshop is equally absurd. Some commercial compounds in which important mineral elements are carried are trouble causers. When such compounds bring about changes in the soil that seriously disturb the microbes, the earthworms, or other beneficial biological life, discord is certain to arise.

According to the well-known biochemist and compost authority, Leonard Wickenden, the greatest injury from the continuous use of chemicals is not so much chargeable to the chemicals per se, but rather to the too rapid solubility of these fertilizers. It is this ability of some compounds to go into spasmodic action as soon as they reach the soil which upsets the delicate balance in the soil's workshop. Some soil chemicals act much like a crazy man armed with a baseball bat who has been turned loose in a glass factory. They tend to wreck things. Furthermore, there are some strong chemicals which break down the *natural* compounds in the soil—the soil's reserve—and bring about the formation of new compounds which lock up the food substances so completely "a sledge hammer can't release them," quoting Doctor Ehrenfried Pfeiffer directly. Locking up the nutrients so they will be lost to the plants is just as harmful as releasing them so they wash out easily.

Applying strong chemicals to weak land where the organic materials are not present in sufficient quantity to serve as buffers, unfortunately a common practice, most certainly is not good land management. There are cases in which a fairly strong initial treatment with a commercial is justified, as stated elsewhere, and that even before the land has been given any sponge structure. On land so poor, for instance, it can't produce a decent crop of helpful weeds or any other type of crop, drastic action may be called for in order to effect revival. Here the elixir will often perk up the dying long enough to permit the biological agents to continue the land on the come-back road. But once these agents are well on the job, the invariable rule should thenceforth be followed: first the organics, then the commercials as supplements when needed, and in the right amounts to *enhance* instead of *obstructing* the activities of the workshop.

I am occasionally asked, "Is not much to be gained by combining natural methods of soil management with an accompanying use of commercial products, even though one is able to follow the natural method completely?" The question is always difficult to answer because there are so many products like guano, slaughter-house waste, bone meal, lime, rock phosphate, and several others which are in every way safe in the soil. Considering the question solely from the viewpoint of strong chemicals versus natural methods of soil fertilization, such a procedure could be made to work and would even be advisable when the maximum of food-production was the goal. I'll go even further and say that it is possible to combine the two so as to get harvests that are abundant without a reduction of quality. There is no denying that, *where the organic content of the land is strong*, one is not likely to go wrong through the use of chemicals, provided he does not overdo in their application. In other words, there are advantages to be gained by tying the most natural methods of soil maintenance to those initiated by man—when there is real and not merely make-believe co-operation. Ample facts support my often repeated claim: commercial fertilizers can be made to have a constructive place in soils where there is a good sponge; chemicals can easily be poison where the sponge is lacking. And to those good folk who refuse to have anything to do with commercial chemicals—you don't need to have anything to do with them provided you have ample materials for building compost, and further provided that you make full use of green manures, barnyard manures, and some each of agricultural lime, rock phosphate, and potash. When you do that, you have Nature right at your side, all the way. *Each in his own way!* Then why the controversy over which is right? Both are right when directed by intelligence.

If those people who are strong for the use of commercial chemicals would first urge a good organic build-up in all land to be thus fertilized, they would not only be advocating correct land management but in time, if they happen to be manufacturers or sellers of such products, would do a more lucrative business. They would be giving with their fertilizers the right kind of guidance—something that is not always true at the present time. If a farmer is induced to ignore the natural and employ the artificial alone, his land will in due course bring him to account, and he will in turn become an antagonist of all commercials. Such a situation will not do our suffering agriculture any good. One can find an abundance of evidence, if he is willing to look for it, that this situation is already coming about, and the refusal of some fertilizer advocates to recognize it is worse than the case of the ostrich with its head buried in the sand. The increasing use of commercial chemicals in the United States as a whole does not in the least change this picture for the better.

With the wide-awake farmer the question occasionally bobs up: "After one has built up his land by the natural method, how much can he additionally improve this land without injuring the biological rhythm that has been established in it?" In such land, the fertility chain will already be functioning efficiently—else the rhythm would not be there. Now the one problem is to retain it. Since every line in the fertility chain will now be on the job—micro-organisms, some fixing nitrogen, some fixing minerals; the molds and algae processing food materials—there isn't much more that can be asked or that can be required. In such a soil the earthworms will take care of mineral circulation in reasonably good shape, even though the friendly weeds are not permitted to take part. So why look for more? This is the soil that will give a harvest of health-sustaining foods and give them in abundance. This, really, is the acme of good farming.

"But my land is far from the type you describe!" somebody else retorts. "My soil is really poor! Besides, Nature takes too long to repair soils in the way you describe. Furthermore, not only are my own soils worn out, but most of the soils I know anything about are sick. And the world is calling on us for food. Above all we need *quality* food. How are we in America going to meet those demands unless we improve our soils in the quickest possible way—which is with commercial fertilizers? Composting and the like are all right on small areas, but isn't it sensible to use commercials where the acreage is extensive, as on our large wheat farms?"

Where the commercials are *correctly* used, the answer to the last question is emphatically yes! And one should not get a wrong impression here: using commercials *correctly*, as described in this book, is *co-operating with*

Nature. Farming with Nature is just as feasible on large acreage as on small areas. The trouble is that most people refuse to learn just what farming with Nature really is. Anything or any operation which *enhances* the activities in the soil's workshop is farming with Nature. But merely speeding up those activities is not necessarily enhancing them.

Many years ago there was organized on the West Coast a concern known as the Western Soil Bacteria Company. The head of this company, C. F. Pennewell, was both a humanitarian and a soil scientist of the very highest caliber. The policy of the Western Soil Bacteria Company was to sell service along with its WESTROBAC, the culture it manufactured and sold for inoculating legumes. The price charged for "inoculating an acre" with Westrobac was eight times that normally charged for the culture sold by some concerns. But with every purchase of Westrobac went scientific guidance that was not based on guesswork. Farmers were taught exactly how to improve their soils the Westrobac way, and a guarantee of satisfaction went along with this service. Every field representative, whether an agricultural graduate or not, was required to complete definite courses in the Westrobac school before he was given charge of a district. The field man had to know how to farm the Westrobac way, and he had to be able to sell the system to the co-operating farmer. The Westrobac Company did what the agricultural colleges should have been doing, but weren't.

I can envisage commercial fertilizer concerns of today pursuing a Westrobac course: intelligent service with every fertilizer sale. Farmers would welcome such trust-worthy guides as they welcomed the Westrobac men. Un-fortunately the commercial fertilizer concerns as a rule do *not* have men in the field who have had the intensive type of training I describe. Very few agricultural college graduates are qualified for the assignment here envisaged. But the fertilizer companies could establish their own schools as we who were associated with it established the Westrobac school. They could train their field represen-tatives to have the Nature concept of land management— and then fit their commercials into the natural way of doing things. This program could become extremely ad-vantageous to them.

No strong chemicals until the sponge structure is well established in the land; then just the right kinds and right amounts of fertilizer for each specific case. Why not? This plan would inevitably bring together a very essential group of agricultural workers: the fertilizer representa-tive, the county agent, the representatives of U.S.D.A., the farmer—and Nature. Thus we have intelligent co-operating individuals with Nature taking the lead. Such an operation can be made to work for the good of all— carried to every corner of our land.

There are now strong indications that, before we can ever hope to rebuild the soils of the world to the point where they will be rich in health factors, the sea will have to be called upon to return what it has stolen from the land.

Most people think of the "salt of the sea" as being nothing but sodium chloride, or common salt. This, however, is far from the fact. Sea water is particularly rich in many of minerals and trace elements often mentioned in this book. Indeed, some of the latter are found abundantly only in the sea. A well-known food specialist has used pure sea water as a fertilizer with marked success, and predicts that it will not be long before "sea salt" takes its place as a fertilizer essential.

But at the present moment our logical source of the trace "accessory foods" is probably seaweed. Processed seaweed as a reliable plant food is no longer theory; it is fact. I have personally made tests with this seaweed product that far exceeded my expectations. I have found that a small quantity of seaweed fertilizer will go a long way in fertilizing land, because only minute quantities of the trace materials—iron, copper, zinc, manganese, boron, and molybdenum—are necessary, compared with the major mineral elements, in maintaining a dynamic fertility chain. While we need further tests—many of them to be exact and under all types of conditions—before definite statements can be made as to the correct acre applications, my own tests indicate that fifty pounds of seaweed fertilizer are normally ample, and anything over one hundred pounds may prove excessive.

In any case, the briny sea probably holds within its bosom one of the vital treasures for a healthy soil.

5

Plant Life Within the Soil

THE plants that live and work completely within the soil consist almost exclusively of the fungi and those tiny green plants called the algae. The latter were discussed briefly in connection with green manures. Botanists uniformly include the bacteria or microbes in the plant kingdom, but passing over the question whether or not they belong there, we are giving a separate chapter to the soil germs later on. The soil microbes are, of course, intimately associated with the fungi or molds, as they are with the algae. Each has an important job to do in the soil's workshop, along with all the other agents which constitute links in the fertility chain. Though the earthworms and the microbes and many insects have long been recognized as essentials in a living, productive soil, the molds and algae have only of late years been accepted as equally important. It has now been proved conclusively that when this fertility link is completely lacking, some groups of plants are unable even to start growth.

Probably the most important member of this link in the fertility chain are the molds, of which there seem to be several kinds. Half a century ago practically all molds that lived entirely within the soil were generally looked upon as enemies of crops, and indeed some of them were and still are. However, the injurious soil fungi are insignificant as compared with the beneficial groups. In the period when molds were still suspect, moldy dirt was passed off as poisonous—as bad as "toadstools." Such soil was almost synonymous with a root disease of some sort.

Not all farmers in a forested region were of that opinion, we are happy to remember. There were always those wise men of the woods who knew the value of forest mold, because they were forever having occasion to prove its worth. To a true woodsman-farmer, any claim that the dirt from his beloved woods could ever be harmful just didn't make sense. Men of his persuasion didn't know just why the spongy earth, built from the decay of hackberry and elm and hickory and oak leaves, was so good, but they did know that their gardens produced more bountifully when the soil was treated with rotten leaves odorous with mold. This was evidence enough that the leaf-dirt possessed virtues of a special kind.

Now we call this mold. The word mycorhiza actually means the association of a fungus with the feeder roots of a higher plant, to the benefit of both. At present the word is generally accepted as the name of the fungus, or group of fungi, which live on the roots of plants and thereby help the plants in several ways.

During recent years several scientists have done much in the way of mycorhiza investigation, but the English scientist, Sir Albert Howard of compost fame, did more before his death than all other investigators combined to reveal the constructive place of this mold, or groups of molds, in maintaining a healthy soil fertility and consequently a healthy plant growth. Because of Sir Albert Howard's penetrating studies, the fungus once considered detrimental to crops now ranks among the indispensable great. The famous drug, penicillin, is often associated with the mycorhizas, but is not one of them. It is entirely probable that mycorhiza will in time be honored far more even than penicillin as a health factor, due to the fact that mycorhizas play a day-to-day role in the production of food, without which disease itself becomes of strictly secondary importance.

Nature often works in ways that are not easy to understand. Sometimes the very simplicity of her operations makes the comprehension of them most difficult. Sir Albert Howard must have been awed when his investigations first opened to him the door of mycorhiza secrets, for they were indeed secrets at that period. This fungus had been a stubborn problem. Save for a few isolated scientists, it was believed until Sir Albert Howard's discoveries to be a poison in the soil. Abruptly it was found to be absolutely essential to plant growth.

Instead of killing plants, or poisoning them with its hyphae or threads entwined around the rootlets, the mold was actually discovered to be carrying food materials directly into the plant. Moreover, before the substances were fed to the plant they had been improved by the fungus, thus making them more assimilable. We must not get the impression, however, that this mycorhiza association with crops enthrones the mold as an angel of unselfishness. Far from that. Wherever it grows, and in all its operations, the mold looks after its own interests first. While it feeds the plant, at the same time it takes from the plant certain nutrients which it needs. In nature the equation is balanced, but from the point of view of man's needs, the crop gains most. This is another full demonstration of natural co-operation; a symbiotic relationship from which both the mold and the host plant benefit—and man probably reaps the greatest benefit of all. At least it is within man's power to do so.

Though there is still much to be learned about this now famous mold, despite Sir Albert Howard's numerous contributions, it would seem that the mold's greatest value in practical agriculture comes from its ability to gather up food materials for the higher plants where these materials are otherwise practically unavailable, and then feed the materials to crops very much as the crops need them. The fungus tubes or threads which force themselves into the tiny, super-sensitive roots of the host plant are themselves extremely delicate, also highly nourishing. After serving as food channels for a period, the threads are absorbed by the host as a food. And as the old hyphae are absorbed new ones are grown to replace them. The process continues indefinitely unless the fungus environment is destroyed in some way.

Long before he had completed his investigations, Sir Albert Howard became convinced that the mycorhiza mold is responsible for much of the good work going on in the soil's workshop that has been ascribed to other soil agents. One more of the mold's several excellent qualities is what seems to be its special ability to collect minute particles of phosphorus in soils where a chemical test reveals a weakness or complete absence of this element. Since phosphorus is one of the mineral elements that constantly calls for attention by farmers, this work of the mold stands out as being more than ordinarily valuable. Sir Albert believed that this one activity of mycorhiza would ultimately bring the mold into universal recognition as a necessity in growing high-quality fruits, vegetables, choice flowers, and other ornamentals, as well as many common farm crops. This is because the mold not only accumulates phosphorus but as has already been pointed out feeds the phosphorus directly into the plant, in a form which permits its assimilation.

The ideas expressed in the above paragraph flow directly from the work and writings of Sir Albert Howard. They need much additional experimental work for confirmation, although we already know that, in soils deficient in phosphorus, the presence of mycorhiza sometimes is accompanied by plant growth which in no wise reveals phosphorus deficiency. There is room here for an inference, which, however, ought not be made until exhaustive tests will permit it to be spelled out.

The idea has also been expressed that mycorhiza is, additionally, a "fixer" of both phosphorus and nitrogen. That is, it is supposed to be able to take both of these essentials to plant growth from the air and process them for use by the more complex plants. This idea is without corroborating experimental data, to my knowledge, but

I would not reject it out of hand on that account. Admittedly, however, the amount of phosphorus in the air is almost too small for recognition, and if mycorhiza takes it from the air, it has done a service which is remarkable in an already remarkable plant world.

Sir Albert's studies led him to conclude that legumes grown in soil rich in mycorhiza did not to any extent produce nodules on their roots. The legumes in mycorhiza-rich soils obtain their nitrogen from mycorhiza fixation and from the supply of nitrogen fixed by the free-living bacterial groups. In his book, *The Soil And Health*, Sir Albert states succinctly: "The root nodules are only a device to save the legumes from nitrogen starvation."

When more of the facts are known, it will probably be discovered that there are several strains of mycorhiza that in some manner aid plant growth, and through the plant benefit the animal. Sir Albert recognized at least two strains, one of which does not channel the food ingredients directly into the roots, but only wraps its hyphae or threads around the tips of the very small roots and then operates in that fashion. This latter type, though the threads do not enter the root cells, does seem to improve the nutrients in some fashion before the latter enter the roots in the usual way, that is, by osmotic action. In those cases where the hyphae penetrate the roots, the threads pass from cell to cell, depositing rich substances around or near the nucleus or heart of the cell. Most of this substance, along with the absorbed fungus threads, will ultimately reach the leaf system or other parts of the plant in some form of protein.

Farmers and gardeners who may wish to strengthen the mycorhiza growth in their soils will need to remember that this remarkable mold, like all fungi, must have a strong organic medium on which to live and work. This does not mean that the soil should be mostly organic, as is found on a virgin forest floor, but mycorhiza won't do much in soil that has no sponge at all. In order to carry on the role which Nature has assigned it, the mold must have something resembling its correct environment. But mycorhiza, given reasonably good working conditions, is able to improve not only its own environment but also the environment of the other agents in the soil. Its hyphae, which work actively through the upper layers of soil, serve as food for most living things which come in contact with them. One of the most important discoveries in mycorhiza is that a soil is almost invariably healthy where mycorhiza abounds. Thus mycorhiza is a barometer of health. Health is revealed in the plant which grows in a soil rich in this mold, and in the animals which feed from such plants.

The mycorhiza association is now known to exist in nearly all of our domestic crops—when the soil conditions are suitable to the mold. This association is apparently necessary. Pine seedlings, for example, will refuse to take permanent root in some regions unless there is a reasonably good mycorhiza growth in the soil. Often all that is necessary to secure healthy pines is to dip the seedlings in "mycorhiza mud" before transplanting them. Apples also have a very close affinity for this mold. It was Sir Albert Howard's study of apple-tree roots which first revealed to him the importance of mycorhiza. It is quite probable that many once thriving apple districts in the United States no longer produce good apples—or any apples at all—because the mycorhiza mold no longer exists in sufficient strength in these orchard soils. Erosion or wrong tillage practices, or both, very likely brought about the destruction of the essential mold that flourished in the soil when the orchards were planted. The direct cause of the disappearance of fruit might have been pests or diseases, but as long as the mycorhiza association existed (which is about the same thing as saying, as long as the health factors were thriving in the soil), the apple trees were able to resist their enemies. I personally know of some once fine orchards that were short lived, and I am now certain that mycorhiza depletion was the chief cause of it. Except for a few localities in our country, the apple is not highly resistant to its enemies. And a sick soil is likely to result in a sick apple orchard.

But apples are not the only crop that is highly responsive to mycorhiza. People who get unsatisfactory results with their roses, no matter what they do to improve them, may find that their rose troubles result from mycorhiza deficiency. The rose is a close relative of the apple. The renowned wine grapes of France are grown in mycorhiza soil. Where mycorhiza is not thriving, the French wines are of a much lower quality. In most peach districts in our country, where the trees are grown in soil well inoculated with the mycorhiza mold, the trees are freer from disease than when the mold is weak or lacking. As for strawberries—if one is having trouble putting quality into that much-savored fruit, let him try replenishing his soil mold. Amazing harvests of excellent berries can be gathered from small areas, provided the mycorhiza association is vigorous in the bed. Most cereals as well as garden crops (with the apparent exception of tomatoes) respond to mycorhiza treatment. The same goes for cotton and legumes. When plants become sick, the chances are that the soil also is sick—sick because mycorhiza is not on the job and functioning efficiently.

Nothing will put mycorhiza into the soil more satisfactorily than good compost. Correctly built compost, after it has stood a while in the open, soon develops a vigorous growth of the mold if it remains moist. Sheet-composting will also bring mycorhiza into the land and retain it if this method of soil management is carried on persistently. There are other ways of establishing mycorhiza, too: livestock manures used regularly, and green manures when made a continuous part of the rotation. In fact, a good sponge structure is a natural mycorhiza environment. When its environment is right, the mold will move in of its own accord in most cases.

Of course, we should not forget that a good inoculation of forest soil is enormously helpful where such soil is available. Well-rotted livestock or poultry manure, richly treated with leaf mold and the mixture applied in the autumn, is the very best treatment for an anemic rose garden. Maybe one is so situated that he can inoculate his compost and thus give that extra mycorhiza strength before applying it to the soil; or mix forest mold with barnyard manure where the latter is to be used on fruits, flowers, or vegetables; or, as my mother did, apply the forest soil directly to the vegetable or flower plots.

And now an urgent reminder—too much lime in the soil will weaken the mycorhiza or even destroy it. While the soil's microbes can endure a fairly high lime content, the beneficial molds cannot. Which is to say, the molds want a soil that is slightly more acid. As the soil chemist puts it, the *pH* factor is not the same for these two vital fertility links.

The fact that legumes are fairly heavy lime users has given farmers, and many soil scientists also, a wrong lime concept respecting crop soils. Seldom does anyone stop to realize that it is easier to apply too much lime to the land than too little. Our calcium standard for cultivated soils is a bit too high. It is true that where green manures are grown extensively, lime is necessary to keep the excess acid under control. But a small amount of lime will go a long way even for this purpose. Pouring lime onto the soil at the rate of two or three, or even four, tons per acre, save for an exceptional case here and there, is employing lime too heavily. The beneficial molds can't take it and the microbes will do better with less—and so will most legumes. We need a new slogan: LESS LIME AND MORE MYCORHIZA IN OUR FOOD-PRODUCING SOILS.

Though mycorhiza is unquestioned queen of that plant world within the soil, we must not get the idea that our algae are not also vital in maintaining an unbroken fertility chain. Since chlorophyll-bearing plants can live and work only where there is considerable light, the algae— the microscopic food makers down there under our feet

—need a soil that is well aerated, moist, and comparatively warm. A soil with considerable fiber in it, in other words. In a moist, mellow soil, the algae, because of their enormous numbers, manufacture food in very considerable quantity, and they do their work just as efficiently, considering their size, as the acres of green leaves with which we are all familiar. The food produced in these tiny food factories, especially the protein compounds, are important sources of nourishment for the microbes and possibly for the molds too, though the latter are more likely to call on the algae to share with them their sugars and starches.

Here once again Nature is doing a harmonious and indispensable job. The molds and the algae and the microbes are all working harmoniously together, each lending much of importance to the existence of the other—and the result is a workshop without discord unless man interferes. Each of these workers also builds and processes for the vast world of higher plants; and each builds and processes for us. Death and decay are as persistent in the soil's workshop as are birth and growth. But there is still no loss, for each of the dead algae is a speck of protein ready to be absorbed by the roots of domestic crops. While algae probably do not perform as many intricate tasks as do the molds, they have their niche to fill, one of which is, as we have also discovered, where land is heavily cultivated. Hence the importance of young green manures.

Along with the microbes and molds, many algae are known to be nitrogen-fixers, at least to a limited extent. Nature, it can be seen, is forever about the business of maintaining a nitrogen supply! The algae, quite likely, consume most if not all of the nitrogen they fix, in producing some form of protein. In a good soil these specks of protein, coming from both dead algae and dead microbes, probably have considerable bearing upon the maintenance of the soil's rhythm.

Workers unseen and largely unsung—this is the truth about the plants within our soils; but it is they, assisted by the microbes and earthworms, which put quality into our grains, vegetables, and fruits—and into our animal products as well. And as a final word to flower growers: a soil rich in mycorhiza will put brilliance and character into your blossoms as will no other treatment.

6

Microbes of the Soil

TO discuss any subject as technical as soil bacteria in a manner that will appeal to the lay reader—that is very close to a task colossal. But it would be impossible to discuss the soil without referring to the soil's microbes. Without the contributions of these infinitely small organisms to the soil's workshop, there just wouldn't be any soil as we understand that term in agriculture.

Whenever the word bacteria is mentioned, the connotation of disease is carried to most people. There are, of course, many kinds of disease-producing bacteria, but far more important to us as humans are the beneficial microbes. It would require many chapters to tell about all the good which the different groups of soil microbes do for us. Some soil scientists even consider the microbes of the soil the only *reliable* barometers of a soil's fertility.

And soil scientists are not far wrong in this respect, for it is these countless millions of helpful soil germs which are largely responsible for the many transformations and biological operations that are continuously going on in the soil's workshop, where some of the most important nutrients are processed for the food factory in

80

the leaves of growing plants. Practically all chemical changes that take place in the soil are under the influence of the microbes, even though enzymes have much to do with these changes. Since the activities of the microbes are so diversified, it is only natural that there should be many strains of them working harmoniously together—and all of them indispensables in maintaining the rhythm in productive land, precisely as is the case with the molds and algae. The operations of all of them are essential to the production of the food materials necessary for the support of healthy organic life.

Study of the microbe populations in the soil by means of the microscope, cultures, etc., can often tell more about the soil's needs than can be obtained by chemical analysis, particularly when the study extends to and includes other plant life and the earthworms within the soil. Such a biological study can reveal the mineral needs of land particularly, for almost all microbes are heavy users of minerals, notably sulfur and phosphorus. The microbes will be comparatively weak where the *supplementary* or trace mineral foods are seriously lacking. On the other hand, if the microbes are thriving, they are probably getting all the minerals they need, and this likewise means that plants growing on such soil are probably sufficiently supplied.

Farmers, it goes without saying, are not in a position to make this complete biological analysis of their soils, but neither can they completely analyze their soils chemically. Government agencies *should* be qualified to make biological analyses, very much as they make the chemical ones, but since this is rarely the case, there are many simple yet practical ways of measuring the soil's strength in terms of its microbiological activity. Some of them were discussed in an earlier chapter, and they are worth remembering. The natural signs of a soil's richness are clearly evident to anyone who is observant. Many things point to the much desired soil dynamics which should always be the farmer's goal. One can learn to recognize soil aromas, for example, for which molds and microbes are both responsible. You do not find these satisfying aromas eminating from a soil that is eroded or otherwise depleted. The earthworm population is an indicator, too. If the fishing worms are present in great numbers and are busy and energetic, you can depend on it that the microbes are there also, and healthy. In all my study of soils I have never found a case—that is, where I made a close study of it—where earthworm strength did not reveal beneficial microbe strength. Finally, we have an elusive but definite test in the spongy feel of good soil, a test which an experienced hand does not mistake. To be able to read soil with the hands is an art well worth cultivating.

Where do the beneficial microbes come from that are needed in reviving "dead" land? A good question, that; but in even the poorest soil some strains of useful microbes continue to exist, ready to revitalize the situation. Nature is alert to take care of that. It's a desperate soil that harbors no good microbes at all. These germs respond and multiply at an enormous rate as soon as the right kinds of food materials are made available in their habitat. In this, they are like other, larger species. The essential germs are also put into the soil when organic materials like barnyard manures and compost, and to a considerable degree, green manures, are utilized. In the process of thus restoring fertility to the land, the fertility links are once more made operative, and, most important for immediate purposes, the microbe link grows stronger inevitably.

Since practically all of the beneficial microbes feed on organic matter in one form or another, once these decaying or decayed plants and plant materials are inoculated into even the poorest of land, the microbes soon are present in sufficient numbers to effect a vital change in the character of the soil. All of which takes us right back to one of Nature's fundamental blueprints: a working sponge structure. A good sponge never fails to enhance microbe multiplication, and the more varied the organic materials which go into the soil for building the sponge, the more satisfactory will be the microbe environment.

Harmful bacteria, as well as beneficial ones, now and then infest soils—farmers and gardeners will have to face this possibility. Disease-producing bacteria are often attracted by the same living conditions that are required for our helpful strains of microbes. Even so, healthy plants are normal and sickly ones are not. It is a normal operating procedure to see the strong survive. This is a phase of natural selection. Man will do well to help, not hinder, the process. Some months ago I saw a fine demonstration of this. A farmer whom I visited was growing an excellent crop of potatoes, and without a single visible potato bug in his entire potato plot, though he had done nothing to the crop other than to give it very meager tillage. Not far from this man's field were other potato patches, and every one of the latter that I saw was lousy with potato beetles. Some of these crops were completely defoliated, despite the use of insect-killers in some instances. But the soil in the first field was Nature's soil in the truest sense, having been built with compost along with other natural treatments. Most of the biological indicators were strongly evident in that soil. The soils in the other fields were almost completely the reverse. There was not the slightest indication of the presence of natural health factors.

It is a promising sign that such examples as that field of insect-free potatoes are no longer the exception they were a few years ago. Many farmers and gardeners are now discovering that strong natural soils, naturally maintained, put into plants an added vigor which gives them the power to resist many insects and diseases. Without doubt, the microbes have much to do with the development of conditions essential to natural resistance. There are other factors which are as necessary as microbes in providing the essential conditions here described, but the microbes will probably be found to be Nature's chief warriors when all the facts are known. Among these other factors is the previously described mycorhiza, the "penicillin of the soil," as it is sometimes called. No one can deny that mycorhiza stands well towards the top in maintaining a vigorous fertility chain, and earthworms are not far behind.

When, as farmers and gardeners, we keep in mind how much the soil's microbes can do for each one of us, and equally for the populations of the world not directly concerned with the soil, we can more easily associate the word germ with the good things of earth—and with the beauty of earth, as well. Food or flower—there is no difference, for the soil alone can give them true quality. This, fundamentally, is the reason for developing those conditions of fertility in land which are manifested in good crops and fine flowers. Back of these manifestations is the more fundamental reality, often neglected because it cannot be seen. It can, however, be understood.

We are all familiar with the microbes which bring about decay of organic matter. They constitute some of our most valuable allies in the maintenance of both the soil and the human habitat. If it were not for the germs of decay, the living would have to move off the earth to make room for the dead. We can therefore be grateful that, in the natural order of things, whenever organic life comes to an end, disintegration must soon follow. It is thus that waste of essential materials is held to a minimum. The dead structures, under the influence of certain bacteria, fall apart and give back to the soil and air most of the elements drawn from these realms in the first place.

In the decay process, which is forever at work about us, many groups of microbes are involved, each group performing a distinct and specific task. Beginning with the coarser plant tissues, step by step, with a different group of germs taking over at each step, the plant bodies are disintegrated completely, until there are left only organic compounds or free elements which return either to the air or remain in the soil. In this systematic and harmonious progression of organic decay, we have a fine illustration of the division of labor in Nature. Nothing in the human mechanical world can approach it.

But so much for the work of decay. In the soil there are also many groups of microbes engaged in building up plant life instead of tearing it down. The former are hardly more important than the latter in the life cycle; it is merely that we are partial to the germs that help us specifically to live. The nitrobacters are one of these groups, and they are wonderful friends of the farmer's. They transform certain nitrogen compounds into other compounds that can be used easily by crops. In the first several inches of a good soil, the nitrobacters are numerous and work like pumps to keep the available nitrogen moving. Those who have studied the soil's microbes closely have discerned nitrobacters in the film of water from which the plant roots absorb their nutrients, and in great numbers. Since every dead microbe is a speck of protein, it is not difficult to see how valuable even one drop of soil water can be—provided the soil in which that water is found is of high quality.

Then we will recall the nitrogen-fixers discussed in connection with green manures. Actually, these nodule-builders are not nearly as important in maintaining soil fertility as we have long thought them to be. Here is an even stronger statement about them by Sir Albert Howard than the one quoted in an earlier chapter: "Agricultural colleges," he says, "are wrong in telling farmers that root nodules will look after nitrogenous manuring. . . ." Sir Albert was convinced that the molds and algae, along with the nitrogen fixing groups of bacteria which live on the soil's organic matter, such as the azotobacters, should receive almost all the credit for keeping up the nitrogen supply.

But this controversy over the relative merits of the several groups of nitrogen-fixing germs in the soil must not cause us to forget some other important groups, among which are the mineral-fixers. We can't let the nitrogen-fixers, vital though they are, rule the whole "food show" in the soil's workshop. There is a region in Africa where the sulfur-fixers are reported to be more active in the soil than the microbe groups involved in nitrogen fixation. These "sulfur germs" have been brought to Europe and put to work fixing commercial sulfur and are said to be doing an excellent job of it. Sulfur is one of the required mineral nutrients, consequently it is safe to conclude that the sulfur-fixers are found in all normal soils. Some scientists are now predicting that the day is not far off when the inoculation of the soils with sulfur-fixing microbes will be recognized as a necessity.

And now we have pretty definite evidence of phosphorus-fixation in land. And according to present indications these phosphorus-fixers are even more active in the soil than the sulfur group. Dr. Ehrenfried Pfeiffer, through his phosphorus investigations, has given us much information on the natural methods by which phosphorus needs of the soil are met. As we know, neither animals nor plants can live without phosphorus, and all soil germs demand phosphorus as "working nourishment" to a relatively high degree. If phosphorus does hold the secret of life, as ancient philosophers believed, then Nature can be expected to have means of assuring its presence in the soil and in sufficient abundance for normal plant growth. Dr. Pfeiffer found sulfur in snow, which *might* indicate a source of this element, though a meager one, far out in the atmosphere. He has also discovered that the soil's phosphorus supply fluctuates very considerably throughout the year, which is pretty clear evidence that the microbes have something, if not all, to do with the availability of this mineral.

On one particular field that had been cropped to wheat for ten consecutive years, and which had given a heavy crop every year, Dr. Pfeiffer reports that soil analyses revealed a different phosphorus content during different months, though no fertilizer other than organic applications was given to the land during the ten years of cropping. And at the end of those ten years the field was a bit stronger in phosphorus than it had been in the beginning.

It is true that the added organic materials had put some phosphorus into the soil, but not enough to feed the crops that this noted scientist took from his land, even though the phosphorus required by the growing plants, was small in quantity. More phosphorus than was supplied had to be found, and the microbes took care of the need efficiently through fixation.

We cannot leave this nitrogen discussion without mentioning something more about Nature's nitrogen cycle.

The natural world is full of cycles, but the nitrogen cycle is one of the most remarkable. Briefly, it consists of the process by which nitrogen compounds are changed and altered. But when we realize that a different group of microbes takes over at each step, the complexity of the cycle stands out with scientific brilliance. Nitrogen, in the organic world, may take the form of protein, which is itself a "nitrogen molecule," which, on finally reaching the end of life, disintegrates and releases its nitrogen to start all over again. From complex nitrogen compounds down to simple compounds—this is the normal process in decay. But in the course of the nitrogen cycle there are also germs operating which *denitrify*. That is, they change fixed nitrogen back to free nitrogen. This free nitrogen returns to the atmosphere and is lost until it is corraled and fixed again by the nitrogen-fixing germs or some other of the soil's nitrogen-fixers.

There is one other outstanding piece of work carried on by the soil's microbes which is too often overlooked, even by those who have some knowledge of soil bacteria. This is a very intimate association existing between the roots of growing plants and certain beneficial microbes. While this relationship is found to a degree with all plants, it is especially strong between the microbes and many weeds. Here is an important reason why weeds can be turned into assets in maintaining the fertility of soils. The benefit derives from the fact that all plants exude substances from their roots. Not all of these exuded materials appear to be relished by the germs, but some of them are, as revealed by the enormous number of healthy microbes which are almost invariably found in the soil close to the roots of particular plants. One does not need a more logical reason for not slaughtering all weeds indiscriminately. By so doing a farmer can weaken his land and lower his crop production just when he thinks he is doing the opposite. Wherever weeds can be permitted to grow for a while before they are worked into the soil, it will be found that they render a service to the soil that farmers and gardeners cannot afford to ignore.

One day many years ago, C. F. Pennewell, the President of the Western Soil Bacteria Company, announced to a group of his field representatives: "Our Westrobac is beyond doubt the best culture for legume inoculation in this country, yet we have made only a beginning in our work with soil bacteria. Our next step is to work towards the improvement of the other soil germs. I am convinced that the productive power of soils is dependent on several groups of bacteria. The nodule-formers are but one of these."

Pennewell did not live to bring his prophecy to fruition, unfortunately for the world's agriculture. But constructive thought never dies. I have just read a paper explaining how a far-seeing bacteriologist, after having collected many strains of soil germs from many parts of the world, has established a bacteria farm on which he is propagating bacteria for the purpose of inoculating land, and is having considerable success with his venture.

Bacteria, like most other living things, can be improved through selection. We did it with Westrobac, the nitrogen-fixing bacteria for inoculating legumes. The work now being done by Dr. Pfeiffer in transforming garbage into superb compost-fertilizer through the use of his "pedigreed" microbes is another illustration of what can be done along this line. This simple though scientific system of salvaging waste and turning it into an asset is the most hopeful sign that has appeared on the agricultural horizon in many a decade. Anyone who doubts the feasibility of improving bacteria needs only to visit one of Dr. Pfeiffer's compost plants—or his laboratory, if he is so fortunate as to receive an invitation to do so—to get an eye-opener that may change his ideas. Or even better, let him purchase a bit of the culture and try it on his own garbage according to directions.

Dr. Pfeiffer, through selection and re-selection, has obtained strains of microbes which, when turned loose in organic matter under correct conditions—garbage, vegetation, barnyard manure or what have you—simply devour the stuff and reduce it to velvety mold in an amazingly short time, as compared with what is required when Nature follows her normal course in bringing about decay. The possibilities of the Pfeiffer system of composting refuse and other similar materials apparently have no limit. What a difference this can make in our hungry soils when farmers as well as city dwellers and city legal authorities awaken to those possibilities!

The main thing that Nature asks of us as tillers of her soils is that we provide suitable environments for the helpful workers she has placed at our disposal. The microbes themselves will do the rest. Through building up the organic supply in his soil, and through applying mineral fertilizers where Nature is not able to take care of them alone, the farmer and Nature join hands—and accomplish things. The more efficiently the farmer or gardener handles his organic materials, the greater the service he will get from his microbes. But as with everything else, mediocre care will bring mediocre results. Whether he is gardening on a small scale or farming very extensive acreage, the microbes in the soil's workshop will take care of the nitrogen and phosphorus to a considerable extent where conditions are made right for them.

7

The Barnlot and Soil Fertility

THE human animal, as many another person has remarked, learns but fitfully. We have been a long time
about the business of discovering simple truths. No matter how the manifestations of Nature may appear to us,
there is no waste in the natural scheme of sustaining
organic life. I will dismiss for the moment the wider
ramifications of the principle of entropy, according to
which the old law of the conservation of energy is but
partially true. Nature is always constructive despite the
fact that she may seem desperately destructive at times.
In the harmonious operation of the basic natural laws,
animal discards are an essential part of the life cycle.
These discards must fill their niche in plant growth, and
indirectly in the life and growth of all other living things.
This exacting demand from the animal illustrates the natural law of compensation. In the natural order of things,
every living thing in some way pays for what it receives.

The recognition of this law as it applies to soil management, that is, the use of livestock manures, has existed apparently since man first started to domesticate
animals, scratch in the soil, and grow plants for food.

Today, at the peak of a long course of development, agriculture honors it more in the breach than in the performance. Since sheep and goats were likely the first animals to be domesticated, it is logical to suppose that theirs was the first dung ever to be employed to improve the soil. Until ancient history brings us down to the Roman Empire, our agricultural literature, particularly that pertaining to the tillage of the land, is meager. One does get a tiny bit here and a suggestion there, and so far as I have been able to interpret what I have found, the employment of livestock manure as a fertilizer for the land was the exception rather than the rule. Ancient Egyptian agricultural literature, scanty though it is, leaves the impression that livestock waste was not uncommonly used to improve the soil, but the Nile bottoms were always so well taken care of by the river's overflows, which always left behind them a thick blanket of rich silt, that there was little need of help from man in keeping up the fertility of the land.

The Nile, a sacred river in ancient times, is fortunate in having its source largely in the tropics, where vegetation is rank. In that period, before modern dams and irrigation canals, an abundance of plant nutrients reached the delta of the river and spread out over the neighboring farmlands during every flood period. Due to the slow movement of the stream and the organic drifts which had their origin in the tropical jungles, much biological life, both living and dead, came from a great distance to enhance the soil's richness in the lower Nile Valley, thus eliminating any large consideration of animal manures in delta agriculture. Whether or not the manures were utilized as fertilizer in the Egyptian uplands, I have been unable to find any record.

Livestock dung in that ancient past, not only in Egypt but elsewhere, was employed as a household fuel rather than as a food for the soil. Actually, in most ancient lands this was the regular source of fuel. The practice is still common in many parts of the world, especially in simple economies. I have found a few isolated cases among primitive farmers in which the dung from the animal yard was used to feed the soil, even where it was normally used also for fuel. But its use as fuel always came first.

In Rome and ancient China livestock manure was considered indispensable in successful farming, and the same is vastly true in modern China. It is a shocking fact that Roman farmers paid greater homage to their compost pits, where they made choice fertilizer from the dung of their domestic animals, than they paid to their goddess of agriculture. These two pits in which the animal waste was given most careful treatment were the ancient means to a soil fertility not always apparent in modern situations. No matter how elaborate a Roman estate might be, every-thing, agriculturally speaking, revolved around those two carefully built pits in the animal yard.

Jethro Tull, the English inventor of the moldboard plow, taught that "tillage is manure." The Chinese, past masters at tilling the soil, know through gruelling experi-ence that such a claim as Tull's just won't work out in practice. Tillage is essential, but it won't fertilize directly. Every Chinese farmer learns the hard way that both livestock and human waste are essential in maintaining his soil's fertility. When the borderline between mere existence and extinction is as narrow and precarious as it is in China, the soil has to be forced to give and give to the utmost. Quantity production must ever be paramount, and it takes more than the very best of tillage to produce the rice for the hungry millions of the Eastern Continent. The Roman farmer, except for the declining years of the Empire, could probably have got along very well without the barnyard waste which he valued so highly. The food-producing soils during the flourishing days of Rome were far from depleted, and the demands made upon them, as long as there were subject nations ready to supply Rome's needs, were not exorbitant.

Therefore, the Roman farmer was in a position to strive for *quality* more than for quantity on his farm. One wonders as he reads the Roman literature if quality foods did not mean more to both producer and consumer during the period of the Caesars than they do in modern times. The manure pits were maintained primarily for the purpose of making fertilizer that would bring land to maximum fertility, because only a soil with such richness would grow the choice foods demanded by the exacting upper class in the cities.

In China, the only ancient nation still existing, I am certain that the use of night soil is not based upon desire, but upon stark necessity. The soil must be fed and fed, and night soil is the only fertilizer abundantly available. Nor does the Chinese farmer carry the soil from his small fields to his corral simply because his ancestors introduced the practice. He does it so that his meagerly fed animals may enrich the overworked earth even a little. The liquid manure from the livestock which would otherwise be lost is too precious to be ignored. Carrying the soil to the corral and back again to the fields means for the Chinese family hours and hours of extra drudgery, but it also means a few more palms of rice at harvest time.

In Europe livestock manure has long been held in high esteem. That is one reason why so many immigrant farmers in the United States almost invariably make a success at farming. They make efficient use of the waste in their barnlots. Once while exploring in Europe I was privileged to witness a neighborhood quarrel over a mere hatful of horse dung. In that particular country, even the animal droppings along the highway were treasured and swept up with care. There was a law governing this which stated quite definitely that the droppings belonged to the farm bordering that side of the road where the manure happened to fall. So, when one member of a farmer's team—when passing a certain farmhouse where this writer happened to be at the moment—deposited a bit of treasure, this farmer dashed out into the road with his basket to make the salvage. The owner of said team, however, insisted that said valuable fertilizer belonged to him since it came from his horse—and hang the law! This led to a vehement argument between the two farmers, accompanied by the waving of arms and the basket. But the law won in the end and no blood was shed, though it looked for a time as though the highway might also be spattered with human gore.

I continued my journey, both amused and amazed. Abruptly my mind was back across the Atlantic at those countless barnlots in the United States where livestock manure and litter were held in such low repute. I knew, of course, that most farmers agreed that livestock manure was good for the soil, yet few ever made effective use of it. And I tried to imagine two American farmers quarreling over one horse's droppings on the highway! Had a farmer been caught in the act of salvaging horse droppings in a public road, he would have been disgraced for life. Even today, with the natural fertility almost gone from our farmlands, livestock manure on the great majority of general farms is still given little more than incidental treatment. Tons and tons of one of the best of soil foods, either when employed alone or combined with some form of compost, is largely ignored.

Fifty years ago, the patrons in one of my rural school districts were incensed because, as they put it, I had the audacity to place in my nature-study course a lesson dealing with the value of barnyard manure. These good people were willing to admit that stable dung was valuable when spread on a field, but why talk about the stuff in public? And it isn't far different today—with some people. Not too long ago I was invited to address a group of women garden enthusiasts on the basic principles of good flower culture. While I was endeavoring to show the high value of decayed poultry manure in building a correct soil for house plants, two members of my audience got up and left the auditorium in horrified haste amidst uncomplimentary expletives.

Our early American colonists no doubt brought with them from Europe a sensible manure concept. But the virgin lands in the colonies where no fertilizer of any kind was needed, or, judged by the abundant harvests, would ever be needed, in time apparently caused a shift in thinking, from manure-appreciation to manure-neglect. But—and it seems that Destiny always orders it that way—there were a few farmers who continued to recognize the value of barnyard waste as their own forefathers had measured it. Many of our foreparents moved the waste from their barnlots to their fields as regularly as they prepared those fields for planting. In every era the few sensible tillers of the soil who refuse to sever their contact with Nature provide the continuity of practice, without which we should retrogress. Wherever such farmers are found, the law of compensation is consistently obeyed—and it is they who are the successful farmers.

Today that school district which objected to my teaching its children the value of barnyard waste is almost deserted. There are few scholars to go to school, and there isn't another McGuffey-minded teacher to teach them. In many respects it was once a progressive district; a well-to-do district for those times. Now it is quite changed. I recall that my enrollment was around seventy, with students coming from numerous, rather than a few large, families. Numerous families meant numerous barnlots—and a staggering number of tons of wasted manure. Whenever I pass through that region now, I have to restrain a tendency to say, even to myself, "I told you so." This is, however, no isolated phenomenon in American agriculture. There are evidences of failure in every section—not from the neglect of the barnlot, but from the avoidance of the obvious.

Some colleges of agriculture pass out the "scientific" information that livestock manure is not what many claim it to be. Most of these manures, they say, are low in the three essentials: nitrogen, phosphorus, and potassium. The spreading of this misleading information, and at the farmer's own expense, is inexcusable, because it lacks foundation in fact. Livestock manure is often low in the three mentioned elements, but carrying them into the soil, even when the manure happens to contain these three elements abundantly, represents only a portion of the manure's total value. Poor soils usually possess little sponge structure, but barnyard manure will rebuild the sponge, and do it efficiently. Any soil without this sponge is still a weak soil, no matter how strong it may be otherwise. *Furthermore, livestock manures are invariably rich in beneficial bacteria.* Even if the manure possessed no other virtues, the microbes alone would justify any reasonable labor and expense involved in its handling.

The value of livestock manures fluctuates, insofar as nutrients are concerned, depending on the kind of animal, its age, and the kind and quality of the food it consumes. Moreover, manures differ in their response when applied to the soil. Manures from horses, poultry, and sheep, for instance, are quick acting, and for that reason are commonly spoken of as hot manures. Manures from cattle and hogs act more slowly and are known as cold manures.

Animals fed a mixture of forage and concentrates, other things being equal, give the richest manure. Animals fed entirely on concentrates give, in the main, manure that is less valuable because it is poorly balanced and the fiber content is low. And certainly animals that have been fed for long on a ration grown on depleted land will not give high-quality manure any more than they will give quality beef or eggs or milk or pork. However, speaking from the standpoint of total values, the quality of the manure fluctuates less with feeding changes than does the value of the main products: the beef, the eggs, the pork, or the milk. No matter how the animal has been fed, the bacteria are always present in manure, and in most cases the sponge value is present, too.

Up until recent years the methods of applying live-stock manures to the land—where manure was applied at all—rarely were such as to get the most out of this valuable fertilizer. It is far better, of course, to apply manure in the rough than not to apply it at all, but not only does the raw manure require an enormous amount of extra labor on the part of those agents of decay in the soil, but there is also considerable direct loss through burning by the sun, leaching from heavy rains, denitrification, etc. With a spreader, and with the spreading being done in the fall or early winter, much of this loss can be eliminated, if the manure can be worked under without too much delay. The spreader can't overcome the extra work required from the workers in the soil's workshop, however, except where the machine is used to spread processed manure. Keeping the manure under cover, and with systematic turning and a little sprinkling with water when needed, much as the Romans used to do it in their pits, is not such a difficult task once the farmer adapts this manure treatment to his routines. Manure thus treated can be worked into the soil any time that tillage is feasible; the nutrients contained in the fertilizer soon go into solution and are thus quickly available to plants. When the weather is erratic and the growing season not the best, this special manure care can mean the difference between a paying crop and no crop at all. Of course, it is in the long run desirable to run the manure through the compost stack, or employ it in sheet-composting. Used in this manner, the manure becomes part of a *complete* fertilizer, that is, a fertilizer more nearly balanced than manure alone.

Some California orange growers are proving in a very practical way that the greatest wealth to be derived from the barnlot may at times be neither beef nor pork, but plant food, just as Columella and Cato, the Romans, taught many centuries ago. These progressive citrus growers have discovered that composted manure applied to the soil in their groves not only raises their quantity production, but it also puts quality into their fruit far beyond anything they were able to get by any other means. Expensive cattle are kept on expensive land—and these cattle at last report were paying off with high profit via their manure. What is being done with oranges in California can be done equally with fruits or flowers or vegetables—or any crop for that matter—anywhere these crops normally grow. The orange growers deserve the highest commendation for their courage and foresight. They are proving that farming with Nature is feasible.

Occasionally doleful complaints come to me, made against unreasonable health authorities in some cities and towns which bar the use of fresh manures on vegetable gardens at or near planting time. These officials are quite right in establishing such regulations. Green vegetables fed fresh manure of any kind, or even livestock manure that is only partly decayed, actually take into themselves certain dissolved substances that can at times cause internal disturbances in human beings.

During the first stages of manure decay, there are released what might be called undesirable compounds which go into solution in the soil water. Dr. Pfeiffer calls these substances a sort of filthy "albumen." Spinach for instance, when fertilized with fresh chicken dung, will absorb considerable of the filth. Potherbs grown on soil fertilized with fresh hog dung just before the crop is planted will, when cooked, send out a strong aroma of the pig pen.

If fresh manure is used in gardens, it should be applied several months before the planting period. But this caution in the use of livestock manures is in no sense a criticism against their use in good farming and gardening. It simply means that, as with other things, there can be a wrong way of making use of a very desirable material. When barnyard manure has been correctly processed or applied to the soil at the proper time, it ranks right at the top with several other quality plant foods.

8

King of Worms

OF the half million or more kinds of animals on the earth, the earthworm is probably the most valuable to man. At first this will appear to be a rash statement, but not when we come to understand how closely human existence is tied to its presence in the soil. There are good reasons for believing that every particle of naturally productive land on our planet has at one time or another traveled the digestive system of an earthworm, because *naturally* fertile, dynamic land cannot exist without an earthworm population vigorously at work throughout the entire surface-soil mass. In the general scheme of things this is one of Nature's irrevocable laws. It is not easy to imagine a headless, eyeless worm possessing such virtues, yet such is the case.

Earthworms perform many functions in the soil, and every one of these operations is vital to the healthy growth of plants. When Jethro Tull, the English gardener who gave much study to the working of soil many decades ago, declared that "tillage is manure" he would have been close to correct had he added, "when the tillage is performed by earthworms." Earthworms are truly Nature's tillers. While prowling throughout the soil in search of food, they churn the soil as no man-made instrument can ever do it. And while they are eating their way through the earth, as a consequence of their ravenous gorging they enrich the soil with their castings while they are improving its structure. And not only is the surface layer stirred and digested, but the worms push their wanderings into the lower soils to a depth of several feet. Without this tunnel-making, root-growth in the lower soils would be seriously hampered for want of air. Not only do these tunnels serve as air channels leading into the subsoil, but great numbers of them are used as highways by roots that would not otherwise be able to reach the moisture below. On heavy soils this is an advantage to many crops far greater than is usually recognized.

But it is the earthworm's ability to add superior fertility to land which lifts it to its pinnacle of greatness. For every earthworm digests its own weight in soil every few hours. The claim that earthworms do not enrich soil directly themselves, but rather are only indicators of the fertility of land, is not based on fact. Countless tests have revealed that earthworm castings are several times richer than the original soil from which the castings were derived. Nitrogen, especially, is very much higher in the castings than in the undigested soil. Furthermore, earthworms, like the molds and some groups of bacteria, are *nutrient accumulators* in the surface soil, except that the worms perform this task far more extensively than do the other agents.

In their foraging through the lower soils, the worms

collect great quantities of primitive nutrients, stuff themselves with these, and then carry them up to the surface where they are deposited as castings within the reach of cultivated crops. These food-building substances lifted from the lower soils are of several kinds and all are indispensables. Among those of special value are the minerals, both the majors and the trace elements. This mineral circulation maintained by earthworms between the upper and lower soils is absolutely essential in maintaining a balanced soil fertility. While minerals can be applied to the soil beneficially, these man-applications can never quite substitute for those provided through earthworm circulation. When we remember, as Darwin the English biologist proved, that as many as eighteen tons of castings are deposited every year in every acre of land that is well populated with earthworms, and that a very large portion of the ingredients which make up the castings is brought to the surface from the lower soil regions, we get a pretty clear idea why the earthworms can rightly be called the king of worms. Any land that can boast this earthworm circulation is sure to be dynamic and charged with health-building factors. Food crops grown on these soils are likely to be healthful.

From the strictly dollars-and-cents angle, earthworms are money-makers for any farmer who will give them a chance to prove it. It would be difficult to evaluate the materials lifted by the worms from the lower regions of the soil, but their money value probably exceeds that of many tons of the best commercial fertilizer. This evaluation is still not taking into account the monetary value of the nutrients which the worms process from materials in the surface soil. True, the worms must be provided organic matter with which to work, but they release richer stuff than they consume.

Darwin was not far from right when he called the earthworm the barometer of soil fertility. Microbes or earthworms—it's hard to tell which are the best indicators. Though this king of worms toils relentlessly for its own benefit alone, all of its labors harmonize with the growth requirements of plants. Here again is a splendid illustration of how harmony in Nature is basic to man's welfare. When the farmer harmonizes his own tillage practices with the requirements of the earthworm, he is working for his own benefit. And he reaps these benefits from several directions. To have the worms enlarge the feeding zone for his crops will often assure him harvests during dry periods whereas his crops might otherwise be complete failures. This particular earthworm value is being proved on many farms today. It is no longer theory.

There seems to be a very close affinity between earthworms and plant roots, and this relationship is not detrimental to plants, as some would have us believe—unless the worms are confined and starved. Earthworms work among roots in order to obtain dead organic materials, *not live roots*. When the worms are confined in pots or boxes with growing plants, they may injure the roots of tender plants if they are not provided extra food. This situation is not likely to obtain in the open where the worms are able to make their escape to more desirable feeding grounds. The castings which the worms deposit around and near the feeder roots are superior pay for the dead rootlets and humus which they consume, to say nothing of the excellent tillage which they do. While this close association between plant roots and earthworms is not strictly symbiotic, in value to the plants it is worth more than the symbiosis which exists between legumes and bacteria—many times over.

Along with other virtues, earthworms are also soil purifiers. In California "pedigreed" earthworms are employed for cleaning up land infested with soil pests. They will eradicate nematodes from a field in a short while. And ravenous eaters that they are, the worms will even devour insect larvae, including sizeable grubs. Recalling that all soil in an area will in time travel the earthworm's digestive tract if the worm population is normal, it is not difficult to see how the earthworm has deservedly been given the name of Soil Doctor by some of its loyal supporters. When a farmer is troubled with a piece of biologically sick land—land that has become sick because of pests and diseases—he should apply weed-fallowing and the earthworm treatment rather than douse the soil with poisons that may in the long run do harm rather than good. Nature's healers, weeds and earthworms, will rarely fall down on the job.

Earthworm farming though not complex must be learned like other worthwhile undertakings. But taking into account all of the earthworm values listed—and there are still others—it is worth all the trouble involved in the learning. Commonly the earthworm population can be built up satisfactorily simply by enriching the soil organically. That is, the worms can be attracted and increased through the continuous application of barnyard manures, correct green-manure farming, or through the persistent use of compost. Sheet-composting will in time change the poorest soil into an earthworm paradise. The worms will in most cases move into the land in droves after two or three sheet-composts.

Native worms can also be transplanted by the farmer from land rich in them, to a field—provided the conditions in the new environment are much the same as where the worms "grew up." This latter factor is extremely important because the earthworm, hardy though it is, is very temperamental. There is a vast number of species of earthworms, each one of which has its own particular habitat and will seldom accept another. The red worm of the manure pile, for instance, will not make a go of it in the garden, neither will the garden worm accept the manure-pile environment.

However, with a little exploring any farmer or gardener can find rich beds of native worms which will accept planting into his vegetable garden or flower garden or orchard, or in boxes or pots. A good place to look for the worms is in mellow forest mold, or around the roots of healthy grass. An abundance of the home soil should be taken up with the worms so as to lessen the shock of transplanting as much as possible. This home soil will also contain many baby worms as well as unhatched capsules or eggs. The latter are more valuable than the old worms, which are very "sot" in their ways. One should study the original habitat of the worms before he moves them. If he will do that and then endeavor to build the new spot—the new home—where he plants them as much as possible like the old, the worms will be more likely to adapt themselves to the new situation.

There is a particular advantage in planting the capsules, which are numerous in all soils rich in earthworms. Whereas the adult worms may refuse to accept the new habitat and either leave or die out, worms born in that soil will accept their new home readily so long as food is available and other conditions are normal. Therefore when making use of local worms to build up his worm population through transplanting, the gardener should make sure to move soil as well as worms, for soil means baby worms and unhatched eggs. Very often the adult worms will migrate if not corraled, despite the best of care, whereas the tiny worms emerging from the capsules quickly accept their surroundings as a permanent home.

Today most gardeners prefer to purchase hatchery worms rather than try to corral and tame the native species. The "hybrid" worms having been propagated under conditions more or less confined, are more docile, and will work more efficiently in restricted areas than will the natives, as a general rule. Most wild worms are wanderers and often are restless when confined. They are always trying to get out and away. It costs little to make a start with commercial worms, and one special point in their favor is that complete instructions for their care, propagation, and use accompany each purchase. This eliminates most of the trial-and-error method, for the beginner will find these instructions simple, yet definite and easy to follow. Though, as already stated, earthworm farming is not complex, some knowledge about it is essential, and the most satisfactory way of getting it is by following the instructions sent out by a reliable hatchery. Many earthworm hatcheries now advertise in certain garden and farm journals. It is good policy to purchase earthworms, or capsules, from a near-by hatchery, if one is available. This eliminates some of the drastic changes for the worms. However, it is better to secure worms from a distant hatchery that is well known and reliable than from one near by that has not yet proved itself.

When one farms with earthworms, he has a right to expect the worms to give him worthwhile returns; consequently there must be no guesswork about the undertaking. And there will be no guesswork if the farmer will approach his problem as he does his other livestock problems. Just like cattle and hogs and poultry, earthworms must have food, and the right kind of food, else they are likely to prove a disappointment. For instance, when the worms are put to work to clean up an infected field, that field must contain considerable organic substance as the basic worm food. That does not necessarily mean that mash or other such material has to be spread over the field as worm food, but it does mean that the field needs to be organically conditioned by means of green manures or animal manures before the worms are planted —unless the field is already organically strong. Indeed, this same procedure is necessary when the aim is to strengthen the worm population in any large field. In case the desire is to plant hybrid worms on large areas, these worms will first need to be propagated in beds or boxes as per hatchery instructions, then disseminated throughout the field, keeping in mind that the living conditions in the propagating bed and the field should be much alike. Under these conditions the commercial worms will multiply rapidly and will need no further attention other than to keep up the organic supply of the surface soil in the field.

In the propagation beds or boxes the worms should be fed the same as other livestock that are confined. Much like hogs, the worms will devour almost anything in the category of food, so long as it does not contain acid or too much salt. In the latter respect earthworms are more choosy than swine. Garbage of all sorts is up the earthworm's alley, and they do particularly well on coffee grounds, stale bread, and meat scraps. One of the most satisfactory foods for earthworms is poultry or dairy mash. The worms thrive on all kinds of mash. They also consume molasses. A feed of syrup, the latter spread on a piece of burlap and this laid on the ground with the syrup down, seems to afford an especially pleasant food situation.

Every farmer and gardener, especially in the country and small towns, should have his general-purpose earthworm bed where he propagates worms for any purpose that may arise. The bed can be any size from a few square feet up. It is advisable to locate the bed in a protected spot, and the soil for it should be enriched with rotten manure or compost, if either is available. This special treatment at the outset is a guarantee of success, though good soil alone will serve when the intent is to feed the worms. On top of the bed should be placed a twelve-inch layer of straw, leaves, or broken weeds. A combination of these is still better, and this mixture should be given a heavy treatment of old manure wherever it is possible. Rotten forest leaves make a superb layer next to the soil in the bed, since earthworms seem partial to forest mold as food. If commercial worms are planted in this bed in the spring, they will soon make themselves at home. Where capsules are planted, one must count on three months before sizeable worms appear.

Should the summer be very dry, some watering will be necessary. As a general rule one will not need to give the worms other care than to maintain the thick, rich mulch on top of the soil, but many prefer to feed the worms also, and find that it pays to do so. Well-fed worms rarely go wandering in search of new feeding grounds. They will roam the subsoil if they are not shut off from it, in search of minerals which they seem to demand. Otherwise they will be abundantly available for fish bait or for planting elsewhere.

A type of earthworm bed is recommended by the United States Department of Agriculture which many are finding very satisfactory. For this master bed, as it is called, a tight box is employed and may be any size to suit the requirement of the propagator. A common size is a box 18 inches deep, 36 inches wide, and 60 inches long. A cover or lid should be provided, and it should extend over the edges to keep rainwater out.

The box should be buried in the ground within a few inches of the top in a sheltered place, and should be shaded from the hot sun of spring and summer. Earthworms cannot endure temperatures above eighty degrees Fahrenheit. The best of good moist soil should be employed for filling the box. A soil well enriched with rotten manure or compost is ideal. After one has planted the worms in the box, he should provide a covering of semi-decayed forest leaves, spread over the soil. During the winter the box should be thickly buried in barnyard manure, to make sure the temperature in the box does not drop to near freezing. During the spring, summer, and autumn, when the worms are breeding, they should be fed occasionally as previously directed. Earthworms multiply slowly unless they are well nourished. And the soil should be kept moist throughout, but never saturated.

Care of earthworms during the winter, no matter what method of propagation may be employed, must receive special attention each year if the earthworm population is to be maintained. While he is a hardy creature, the earthworm has a sensitive skin and apparently is most miserable in a cold soil. In open fields where the soil is deep, the worms will burrow far down into the earth, where they build for themselves very efficient winter homes. Darwin found these winter homes as much as ten feet below the surface, consisting of rooms lined with grass seeds and broken leaves as a protection against the cold earth. In each compartment several worms will roll themselves into a ball, in which condition the winter period is spent in apparent comfort.

Where worms are confined, they are naturally at the gardener's mercy, and provisions should be made to keep them warm in a basement or cellar, or in some similar place. In any case, the boxes should be covered with protecting materials of some sort, such as barnyard manure or straw. It is better, of course, if the containers can be stored in a room where the temperature is under control. Some hatcheries now offer worms, they claim, that will endure zero temperatures. I doubt if any breed of earthworms can stand zero temperature for long. It is better to play safe and make special preparations for winter care. For outside beds, an extra blanket of manure or old straw, applied during late fall, will pay back with an early spring harvest of worms. And finally, one must guard against earthworm predators. One rat will clean out a box on short notice, and ants are even worse than rats. Ants injure indirectly by eating the sugar in the soil. Earthworms must have carbohydrates. These sugars and starches are found in sufficient quantity in a normal soil if ants are not too numerous. So rats and ants must be kept out of all boxes and beds. But caution in the use of poisons, lest more worms be killed than ants, should be exercised.

Even with the advancement already made in earthworm farming, there are those who still belittle the earthworm enthusiast. Such skeptics tend to be more blind than the eyeless worm itself. Darwin was quite right when he declared: "A soil completely abandoned by earthworms is well on the road to permanent sterility." In other words—and repeating—earthworms are an essential link in the fertility chain, which itself must be strong in order to promote a healthy soil. Earthworms are balance factors in the soil's workshop, in that they enhance the powers of the indispensable molds, the algae, and the microbes.

9

Nature and Her Water Cycle

WATER is essential to all organic life. Everybody will agree to this, yet few understand clearly the exact mission of water in the soil. By now we know that the function of soil is to prepare, or provide, nutrients for building food in the plant. According to present knowledge, not a particle of this food material can enter the plant until it has been dissolved in water. Not a single one of the several biological workers discussed in previous chapters—the microbes, the molds, the algae, and the earthworms—can carry on its work unless there is moisture in its working environment, and moisture in the right condition.

Fully to grasp the vital importance of soil water, one needs to view the subject from two distinct angles: water in its relation to the soil itself; water in its relation to the growing plant. Naturally, these two water values are closely tied together. From a practical standpoint, both must be correct or plant growth will be seriously hampered. But with a fairly clear picture of each value in his mind, the farmer or gardener can attack his water problems—or irrigation problems—more intelligently.

Water may appear in the soil in a form detrimental both to the plant and the biological workers in the soil's workshop. This situation may obtain both when there is too much water in the soil mass, and when there is a dearth of it. When such conditions exist, as is the case during heavy rains or during a drought, growth activity is slowed down temporarily or checked completely. Let either condition persist for a long period of time, and troubles of various degrees of seriousness will arise. If the period is one of severe drought, plants will dry up unless they are able to reach out with their roots to some distant water supply, and earthworms will migrate or succumb. Most of the other biological factors will "hibernate" until suitable living and working conditions return, though great numbers of them are meantime destroyed.

Our usual run of plants will starve for water in a flooded soil. This is so because most plants can take in water only from a water film of fairly definite thickness. Actually, except when the soil is completely saturated, water exists somewhat as a film around the soil particles and granules. When this film is extremely thin, as it is in dust, the roots cannot take it up. At the other extreme, such as exists when the spaces between the soil particles are largely filled with water, the film becomes too thick to be absorbed. In a flooded soil the film gives way entirely to a "flow of water," which practically prevents intake by the roots, save in the case of water plants and a few crops that are able to adapt themselves to flooded conditions.

All of this is to say that the water film in our cropping soils must be of an intermediate thickness before crops can make use of it. In soil books, water in this condition is spoken of as "capillary water," which is the water condition concerning every grower of plants when he irrigates, whether he realizes it or not. Since in Nature definite principles operate in regulating this water in soils, a knowledge of these principles is essential to successful farming, whether the farming is practiced in a flower pot or on a vast acreage. Moreover, the best irrigation practices are not necessarily those which are concerned with applying water to the soil by mechanical means. Conserving and utilizing water which Nature offers directly is more important than any form of irrigation.

Permanent, thick water films are, of course, brought to optimum standard through drainage. In many sections of the world water management consists of drainage alone in preventing too thick water films. The thin films in dry regions are brought to optimum standard through various systems of irrigation, depending upon the types of cropping. Contrary to general belief, it is easier to cause trouble through over-irrigation than through under-irrigation. This is a rule that gardeners especially need to keep in mind. Appearances are often deceptive. Too much water is likely to produce a lush growth, but as a rule a weak growth.

Capillary water, that intermediate film which produces regular growth in plants, normally moves through the soil in many directions. When water is applied slowly from above, the films form downward and the moisture moves naturally down to the roots. At the same time this water moves sidewise in all directions. There is a favorable response from all agents of the soil world when water enters it in this capillary form. Flooding the soil, on the contrary, will upset natural balance until the excess water moves on and the capillary film is re-established. Of course, this disturbance is only temporary and the soil agents make up for lost time as soon as conditions become right again. Plants in pots and other receptacles should always be watered slowly; that is, in a "capillary manner."

Land that contains a good sponge structure to a considerable depth will store up much of the excess water and then return it to the surface soil later by means of upward capillarity. Indeed, a soil that is organically balanced has the power to regulate soil moisture. When the organic stuff is almost completely broken down, much capillary water is stored in it and later released for the use of plants. Here is the secret of an efficient soil sponge: water is quickly absorbed as it falls; excess water is sent on down to the water table; a reserve supply is held by the sponge.

A water storehouse in the lower soil is possible only when the sponge reaches to a considerable depth. However, the upward movement of capillary water is not as vital to successful plant growth as it was formerly believed to be. A dust mulch on the soil's surface does help to check evaporation and plants are supported to a degree by this upward moving capillarity. Yet plants seem to go after water rather than wait for the water to come to them. In a soil where there are no serious obstructions, plant roots reach out far and wide. It isn't a case of searching for the water; the function of roots is to reach out for nutriment, and they go unbelievably long distances to get it. Where there is a good, deep sponge, most plants will feed from this lower storage during dry periods. Save in arid regions, it is always better land management to build and maintain a strong soil sponge than to depend in any way on surface irrigation. Irrigation in humid regions will seldom be necessary if the soil is mellow and fibrous to a good depth. It must be kept in mind, though, that coarse organic stuff in the soil *is not a water holding sponge.* The organic materials must be just short of completely broken down.

Returning to the habits of plants to reach out for water, I have traced alfalfa roots eighty-one feet from the nearest alfalfa plants. The alfalfa was getting its water from a shallow stream in a deep swale. I found fruit-tree roots traveling even farther, going under a wide highway and to an irrigation reservoir far out in a field. This wandering of plant roots is a major natural phenomenon. Not only are plants able to survive a long dry spell in this manner, but they are also able to collect many nutrients of which they would otherwise be deprived.

Once the water has entered the plant, it then assumes new duties which are more intimately associated with life and growth. First, the water, after passing into the roots, carries the dissolved materials collected throughout the soil up into the plant where they are needed; and the water itself—or that portion of it which the leaves need—is combined with those nutrients entering the leaves directly from the air. No matter where food building goes on in the plant, water plays a vital part in the operation. The nutrients synthesized by the plant itself have to be transported throughout the plant structure, and water is the carrier. Along with these major tasks, water within the plant regulates temperature and through its continuous pressure within the plant cells it keeps all the green parts turgid and expanded so that the plant can more efficiently carry on other life processes. And finally, as the water transpires from the leaves, it absorbs heat in order to vaporize, thus cooling the surrounding air. From its first entrance into the roots, possibly far down in the earth, until the water reaches the air again whence it originally came, it travels a long and complicated water channel. Of Nature's complete water cycle, this one segment within the plant, the transpiration stream, is probably most intimately connected with our own existence.

This is not to imply that any segment of the water cycle, can be out of order. Water trouble in the organic world can be traced invariably to some improper functioning of the water cycle. Not all water on its way back to the atmosphere, needless to say, must travel the transpiration stream. There are other highways, and these are fully as important as the transpiration stream itself.

Today much of the world is suffering because of weak segments in the water cycle. It is not a case of too much water on the earth, numerous and destructive floods to the contrary notwithstanding. Where floods are persistent, it simply means that one or more segments of the cycle are not functioning. The only redress is to repair the water cycle.

Here let me illustrate with a tragic picture taken from the Cherokee Outlet the consequences of man's disregard of natural phenomena, particularly when he destroys a segment of the water cycle.

We used to call the mile of gurgling springs which emerged from the slope on each side of Mill Creek "the Winding Mile." Some of the springs flowed from beneath giant boulders, while others bubbled from moss-covered or fern-covered banks. Really, it was closer to two miles of meandering creek, bubbling with pure water.

Like a dignified, lazy snake, the creek swept gracefully by the mouths of small valleys and canyons and fairly broad swales, all dotted with gushing springs. On its way to the river, the creek divided many small meadows into halves, each half apparently competing with the other in variation and beauty, especially during the weeks when the redbuds were in bloom and the white plums made snowbanks and the crocuses spread the meadows with their first blossoms. Every so often, after rambling through a meadow, the creek would pierce a primitive forest, but in these places it would shift about as though now under the command of the majestic oaks which lined its banks. Through the thinner woodlands it drove a straight course, much as it flowed through the meadows, until it finally reached the end of our Mile and lost itself in the dense Indian forest of the Cimarron country.

Many feeder branches entered our creek. It was rolling country, and it seemed like stepping from one post-oak ridge to another, if we didn't keep close to the creek as we went downstream. Each of the branches that fed the creek contained bubbling springs up in the draws. The water from the springs kept the water flowing in the creek both winter and summer. I was almost a grown man when I first saw the bottom of our creek bed, except at the riffles.

Now when in memory I survey that diversified landscape along our Mile, with those never-to-be-forgotten springs, and then actually look out over the picture as it really is, and see the barren ridges and the dry creek beds, it is not difficult to understand the cause for the creek's dismal transformation. The creek floods easily now. There was a time when hard rains rarely put the creek out of its banks. Now the creek is either overflowing, or its bed, save for special holes here and there, is gravelly dry. All of which means that the water cycle no longer functions along the Mile; in fact, it has not been functioning for four decades. The springs are practically all gone from the draws. The water that reaches the creek is almost all surface-flow. During even moderate rains the run-off is heavy and the creek must carry it all. Little water soaks into the ground, later to emerge in springs—for there is no sponge-structure in the land.

When the branch streams were numerous and flowing along the creek, our water table was high and our wells were shallow. Our wells used to be twenty to thirty feet deep. Forty feet was a deep well. And the water was always sparkling and cool, like the water in the springs. The water in the great Dripping Spring, the greatest of all our springs, was always cold on the hottest days. Our Master Spring still drips from its giant boulder, but it is now just a lonely landmark; a survival from a past that was so different. Surrounded by oil wells, the old spring seems strangely out of place.

Water tables could stand high along the creek in the old days, because the sponge-filled earth drank in the heaviest rains. There was little surface-flow into the creek and its branches. I have often seen it pour, yet only a trickle reached the creek as run-off. Rainfall, except what fell directly into the branches and the few tiny temporary streamlets, reached the creek via the soil-segment of the water cycle. Except where it ran over barren ground, the run-off after a rain was almost clear. I recall well, for a year or perhaps two years after the opening of the Cherokee Outlet, how we used to go swimming in the creek immediately following or during a rain. Sometimes the creek would come up quickly and rout us, when there was a sure-enough downpour. Ordinarily, though, we went right on swimming when it rained—in almost clear water.

Fifty years ago it was—no, sixty years! When first opened to settlement the Cherokee Outlet was a small oasis remaining in our primeval America. Outside the Indian Territory, the soils of the bordering states were already on the down grade. But in the Outlet the white man found virgin soil equally on slopes and in the valleys. He found fiber-filled soil and an unbroken fertility chain, which gave him abundant harvests of quality produce. These new settlers unfortunately had little sense of land values. Many of them had never before seen a large area of naturally fertile soil. Good folk those pioneers were, but seldom soil-conscious. The distant future meant little to them; the present was too filled with the thrills of pioneering.

The Pawnees were not overly friendly towards these white intruders, nor co-operative beyond what the law required. Often during those pioneer days the Pawnees would watch from the ridges until dusk, then they would gallop back to camp, anger and hatred approaching the scalping point. In their own way the red men loved their creeks and springs of clear water. They were absolute necessities along the winding trails to the Cimarron. The Indians knew almost by instinct what would happen to the springs when the prairies and forests were gone. They could see far beyond the white man's plow.

The transformations that befall a region when the soil segment of the water cycle no longer functions are almost invariably indicated by land depletion. That is now the whole trouble along our Mile and along countless other miles of our country. The soil segment is no longer drinking in the rain where it falls, so the springs have dried up. Wherever there are wells along our Mile, the wells are usually very deep. And it is only now and then that good water can be obtained, even when going to great depth. Rains are just as heavy, though, as when springs were abundant. Records show there has been little fluctuation in the rainfall in half a century. But there are often floods along our Mile now, and the creek overflows into the small bottoms. Some wise ones would tell us that the floods were just as prevalent in the old days. They were not, save during a waterspout. There are still living Indians who know the facts. The soil on the slopes is now sealed except where the land is mostly sand—or where Nature is at her rebuilding here and there. In some places Nature is really at work, yet the task that lies ahead is colossal.

On the whole, just a meandering has-been! And the history and evolution of our Mile would have no place whatever in a book of this kind were it not a warning signal. The watersheds of the Missouri River, together with the river's entire drainage basin, is only our Mile magnified. Exactly the same conditions obtain in all our drainage basins in the United States: the soil segment of the water cycle is not functioning. Even though Nature alone could ultimately rebuild the ravaged segment, our civilization constantly interposes obstacles to that accomplishment. I have heard or read somewhere: "A springless region is a dying region."

Will expensive dams and reservoirs revive springs? Will they put the sponge back into our famished farmlands? Will they repair the broken water cycle in any manner whatever? While the controversy rages the ravages go on. But the natural fact is unequivocal: the only way to bring back the springs, to rebuild the soil segment of the water cycle is to return the conditions as they were when the springs existed. It is doubtful if the large reservoirs can even help to bring this about. But legions of ponds dotting the land would go far in lifting the water tables in all parts where they have dropped so low. But even with great numbers of lakes and ponds, we would still be far from a sponge-filled soil. The water table would rise no doubt, but that would not unlock the surface soil to the falling rain. And only when the surface of our land is opened, only when there is a tiny dam to catch and hold every drop of water as it falls, will the water cycle function and the springs return.

In every virgin forest, where erosion has not taken its toll, the soil segment of the water cycle is usually working at its best. The sponge is alive in such soils. Undisturbed watersheds in the higher reaches, lush meadows— these when they exist are norms. And on every man-made garden spot, no matter how small or large, where all the fertility links are working at top efficiency, the water cycle operates smoothly. But where the sponge is missing and the surface of the land is sealed, as it is today from the Rockies to the Appalachians, tragedy stalks!

10

Nature and Our Foods

NATURE has but one basic food factory. It is in the leaves and other green parts of plants. Animals—all animals, man included—are completely dependent on plants for their nourishment. We cannot manufacture food!

All living things *eat* in order to live. We must have food to give us energy to carry on our physical activities. When we come right down to it, food *is* energy, and the quality and amount of energy we get will depend mostly upon the *quality* of the food we consume. In other words, substances which do not supply us with energy, or which do not help to make use of the energy provided by foods, do not belong to the category of foods. They are merely fillers—or something worse.

Now let's take a peek at just *how* the food factory in the leaf builds food, and also just how it puts the energy into the food during the building processes. As a starter, certain food-making ingredients enter the leaf, the food factory, some coming *directly* from the atmosphere, and some coming up from the soil in tiny streams of water which flow through the plant. These little streams taken together are called, as previously indicated, the transpiration stream. In this first step of food making, practically all of the water used in the processing comes from the soil. The air nutrients consist of a gas called carbon dioxide which, when broken down in the food factory, gives the two elements, carbon and oxygen. The water from the soil usually carries a bit of carbon dioxide, and it joins with the gas coming from the atmosphere to strengthen the total supply. The pure water, when it is broken down, gives hydrogen and oxygen. So now we have three elements out of which the plant builds our basic food: carbon, hydrogen, and oxygen. As we move along the food production line, it is important to keep in mind that this first food developed in the leaf *is the foundation of all other true foods.* All other real foods must contain this basic food.

Most people like sugar, of course, and there is a very natural reason for this, because Nature's basic food is just pure sugar. Yes, the sugar you use on your table is *almost* the same thing, and molasses, and the sugar in fruits. There are many kinds of sugars, but these differ from the basic sugar primarily in the number and arrangement of atoms of these three elements used in their construction. But the most important thing about sugar is its energy-producing quality.

And now this is how the processing is done: The three food elements are assembled in the meshwork of the leaf. Just how this assembling is done is still somewhat of a mystery. We know that the elements come from both the air and the soil, and we know that they are synthesized in the leaf cells. Sunlight, with its limitless energy, is the motive power behind the whole process of synthesis. When this power moves into the leaf, photosynthesis takes place, and this operation is apparently under the management of *chlorophyll,* a substance which is found in small green bodies called *chloroplasts.* Exactly what goes on in the process of uniting the three base elements, we simply don't know. We do know, however, that when the work of photosynthesis is finished we have a molecule of sugar. And it will be helpful to remember that this sugar molecule, constructed in the leaves, provides the foundation of all the other foods that may subsequently be discussed. Fish or fruit, milk or eggs, the sugar elements are their foundation and source.

This brings us to a great group of essential catalysts, the enzymes. Enzymes have been mentioned in former chapters, but now we need to know more about them, most particularly how and where they affect food making. Enzymes are organic substances, neither plants nor animals. They are found abundantly in the bodies of both plants and animals, and are of many kinds, depending upon their organic roles. In building foods, their largest role seems to be to take over where photosynthesis leaves off. The chloroplasts appear to take the place of the enzymes in the first step of food making. That is, the chloroplasts appear to direct the work of photosynthesis, because where there are no green substances there is no photosynthesis. It is known that no chlorophyll enters into the food molecule. So it seems that this green stuff fulfills a general synthetic purpose, without which nothing happens.

But just as soon as the sugar molecule is finished (and here it must be said that enzymes enter into its formation) —which is exactly like saying, just as soon as the photosynthetic work is complete—new enzymes enter the picture and direct the building of all foods from there on. Here is another point at which scientists are not in full accord. Some say that the enzymes actually help to build the food molecule, while others say they are just overseers of the job. In any case, the enzymes in one way or another are responsible for all food including the basic sugar. All other sugars, like grape sugar, cane sugar, beet sugar—all of these are the original sugar modified by the action of enzymes upon it. But the function of enzymes does not cease with the making of food. Enzymes, in fact, direct the digestion of our foods after we get them into our bodies.

But the building of the basic sugar which is so vital to our existence isn't such a mystic operation as would at first seem. Go out into the field and study a growing plant when the sun is shining. With imagination, you can almost see the work of food building going on. Not with the normal organs of sight, of course; yet it is possible to get a mental picture of the steps just described: the carbon dioxide gas from the air pouring through the stomata or doors of the leaf—hundreds of them to every square inch on the leaf's lower surface. Except for water plants that have their leaves resting on the top of the water, or plants growing in deep shade, most leaves exhibit stomata on the lower side. Then one can in his mind's eye see streams of water coming up from the soil, a continuous flow and against the pull of gravity. (A rich soil, with a good sponge which holds the water in the right condition for root absorption, makes a great difference in this water movement.) And we are not forgetting that the water moving up from a rich soil is also carrying other vital materials which are not needed in photosynthesis. Since these do not enter into the base sugar molecule, they will be discussed when and where they are utilized.

Starch, probably the food closest to sugar, is really nothing but the sugar molecule with the three foundational elements, carbon, hydrogen, and oxygen, changed around somewhat. Starch building is more complex and the molecules are larger than is the case with the base sugar. Other enzymes are involved in starch building, and the process takes place not only in the leaf, but anywhere in the plant where the starch may be needed or where it is stored. If one will observe a healthy, fully grown potato plant, he can get a mental picture of starch making. Here he will have photosynthesis and starch making occuring at the same time. As the sugar is constructed in the leaves, it is moved by the plant down to the roots where the waiting enzymes use it to build starch-filled tubers. There are intricate details involved in all this, but the simple picture illustrates fundamentally what happens in the sugar-to-starch transformation.

And next come the fats—still nothing but the sugar molecule with the three elements juggled around by enzymes as was the case with starch. Fat molecules are larger even than the starch molecules owing to the great number of atoms entering into each molecule. Yet fats contain no new elements; just the basics. As should be expected, the enzymes which look after the formation of the fats are different from those which build the starches, but their respective tasks are not materially different. For example, in the peanut the sugar is carried to the developing nut and there changed to fat, and in the castor bean it is changed to our old friend, castor oil. And think of the domestic products built from cotton-seed oil! All of these came from the original sugar molecules which were synthesized in the food factories of the leaves.

And last, though far from least, we have protein. Protein is the food of action and growth. The other foods discussed must provide most of the energy needed by both plants and animals. And protein is more complex than either starch or fat. The three basic elements still form the protein foundation, but now a new atom is added. This atom, which can well be called the dominant atom in protein, is nitrogen—the same nitrogen, after it has been processed, which is most abundant in the atmosphere.

Unlike the three basic elements, since it does not take part in photosynthesis, nitrogen is not permitted to enter the leaf directly from the atmosphere. (Some investigators are now claiming that some nitrogen does slip through the stomata and is "fixed" in the leaf. But for the time being we shall stick to the old theory and hold that it doesn't.) It must travel the longer road down into the soil, where it is given a thorough working over by several groups of microbes, as well as by some of the other soil agents, before it is acceptable in the protein molecule. Why this is so, we are still not sure. But we do know that the soil is responsible for the very large job of working over the free nitrogen of the air into usable food material. Here, for the first time, man is given a chance to do his bit in the food cycle: he can help provide the best possible conditions in the soil where the nitrogen must be processed.

Not only is the protein molecule itself extremely complex, but the method of its formation is not exactly simple. We still do not know all that goes on in its formation, but in general, short-cutting certain technical points, the following may be said:

In the building of the protein molecule of the plant, two distinct steps are involved. The first of these is to combine the foods already discussed, and which are technically spoken of as the carbohydrates, with the fixed nitrogen that has come up from the soil. It seems that this combination can be made with the basic sugar, or with either starch or fat, since they are, after all, fundamentally alike insofar as the chemical elements are concerned.

Now when Nature combines any one of the first three foods—or possibly a mixture of them—with the nitrogen received from the soil, which is now in the form of a nitrate compound, she does not get a complete protein, but a series of acids which chemists call amino acids. The production of these amino acids, which will ultimately be used in constructing a complete protein molecule, is carried on in the plant wherever the protein may be needed, but most abundantly in the young growing parts of the plant. We need to be reminded that this work of building the protein is influenced or determined by enzymes.

Very well, so far we have a series of amino acids—but still nothing like beefsteak which is largely protein. So, as the second step in the protein process, these aminos are now corralled, as it were, and tied together chemically. It is from this union that protein results. It should not be difficult to see how there can be so many kinds of protein in the world. The combining of different aminos, or different numbers of them, will, of course, produce different molecules, yet they are all protein molecules, because they were built by Nature from the same materials and the method of construction was fundamentally the same in each case.

Such is protein. Basic foods plus fixed nitrogen equals amino acids; amino acids plus different amino acids equals protein. And all of this must take place inside the plant. Feed the protein-filled plant or its storehouse of protein to your beef animal, and you have beefsteak. Or eat the plant yourself, and you get the protein straight, as Nature originally intended you should have it.

It is in the protein molecule that we encounter what might be called our only absolute mineral foods. Sulfur seems to form a part of most protein molecules, and the same can be said of phosphorus. It is not clear whether these two minerals should be looked upon as definite parts of the protein, or whether they are merely *accessories* to help the protein do a better job. In either case, whether as food in the absolute sense or as accessories, sulfur and phosphorus are usually in some ways part of protein and no doubt are present for a constructive reason.

And there you have your foods, and, very briefly, the

manner in which Nature builds them. And note, *these foods have been built entirely from ingredients coming from the atmosphere.* Once at the close of a lecture in which I had been discussing the relation between good soil and good food, a man remarked a bit ironically: "Then why all this flurry and fuss about fertilizers and so-called land management? If crops get all their nourishment from the air—and that seems true, for water, after all, is part of the atmosphere—why not scatter the seed on any kind of soil and forget about farming except for a little weeding? The air is the same over poor soils as over rich, isn't it?"

This man's questions brought me up with a jolt. Evidently I had failed to make clear to him some very important points. This, I quickly realized, called for personal instruction immediately. Fortunately there were two near-by fields of corn which supplied excellent material for clearing up much of my critic's confusion. On one side of the highway was a beautiful field that was developing a superb corn crop. The farmer who owned it had built up his land with green manures, barnyard manures, and about the right kinds and amounts of commercials, until his soil was pretty close to optimum. The field on the other side of the road was part of a farm, the owner of which had bought it for its oil prospects. This owner wasn't the least interested in land improvement and gave no encouragement to his renter other than to advise him to mine the land for all it was worth before the hoped-for oil wells eliminated all farming. In the second field the crop surely spoke for itself and for the land likewise. Yes, the same canopy of atmosphere covered both fields—wonderful air, too.

The soil in the first field was truly dynamic. One had only to do a bit of digging to see that. In the other field, though, even the earthworms had died or migrated. If one could have seen the microbes, he probably would have found them gasping for breath, despite all the good air above them. The corn here was sick because the land was sick. The air was on the job but the soil wasn't.

When I saw that my critic still wasn't convinced *why* the quality of the soil in the two fields had so much to do with the quality of the crops, wisdom prompted me to rebuild for him a synopsis of the food cycle, somewhat as I had touched upon it in my lecture, except considerably more in detail.

We must always remember that Nature works in cycles. The food cycle is one of the very greatest, as well as the most complicated, of all of her many cycles. Before we can understand to any degree the *value* of each part of the food cycle, we need to see clearly that values are not measured by *volume*. The same rule holds in everyday human activities. In building a house, we know the nails are as important as the lumber, though there is a vast difference between the volumes of the two building materials. This rule holds severely in Nature's food cycle. The fact that more than 95 per cent of the essential plant nutrients originate in the atmosphere, and less than 4 per cent in the soil, in no sense indicates there could be life without the mighty 4 per cent, which includes the *mineral foods*.

But providing these minerals is only a part of the soil's mission in food construction. True, water originates in the atmosphere, but plants growing in normal soil use only the water which comes to them through the soil. Like the nitrogen in the air, the water in the atmosphere cannot enter the leaves in any appreciable amount. We must remember also the enormous amounts of nitrogen required for building protein. The soil is responsible for the entire nitrogen supply. The growing plant is completely bathed in nitrogen gas, yet not an atom of that gas can be used until microbes, along with the other nitrogen-fixers in the soil's workshop, give it a thorough working over. Without this nitrogen processing in the soil there would be on our planet no protein-filled beans or lean meat—nor any humans to eat them. Better to ask, where *doesn't* the soil enter into the food cycle?

I can still recall the retort from my critic: "Agreed! But *quality* of soil—it's still not clear how quality of soil has anything to do with quality of food!" The good field of corn remains our exemplar. Where do we get quality if not from the soil? The green plant builds practically all of the food which gives it growth. The protein in all the growing parts of the plant must be constructed by the plant itself. A soil with an unbroken fertility chain furnishes the plant with exactly what it needs, and it furnishes the required nutrients in just the right condition and the right amounts. Soil microbes and molds in a well-balanced soil do the kind of job necessary to all of the phases of plant development. The results of this work are reflected in a healthy, vigorous plant. The minute relationships existing between the plant and the soil are far from an open book to us yet, but we know the general outline. We know how to build a soil that will satisfy a plant's most exacting demands—and we know how to collect from the plant all that we need for our own well-being.

And now what about mineral foods? These soil minerals are as vital to our existence as are the sugars, starches, fats—even the proteins. Simply because minerals are classed as accessory foods and are required in microscopic quantities (despite the claims of some to the contrary), compared with the air nutrients, does not in any degree lessen their importance. Just *how* the minerals are utilized by plants, we are still uncertain. We are only certain there would be no living beings without them.

Painstaking investigations have given us valuable knowledge concerning our "mineral foods," notably the work of William A. Albrecht of Missouri and Frank A. Gilbert of the Battelle Memorial Institute, Columbus, Ohio. In plants, for instance, sulfur is known to be a part of the nucleus of cells and also is essential to chlorophyll development. Phosphorus seems essential to healthy roots and stems, but its major work may possibly be as a helper to the enzymes. Potassium aids in the digestion of food in both animals and plants, and there are evidences that this element plays some particular part in cell division and the beginning of growth. Both iron and magnesium enter into the formation of chlorophyll, the iron acting more or less as a sort of "enzyme," while magnesium is a part of the chlorophyll molecule. Calcium evidently performs several important tasks, two of these being to aid in food distribution throughout the plant and to strengthen cell walls.

And of course there are trace elements, many of which seem to be essential to plant growth as well as animal growth. To what degree these rarer elements enter into the life cycle of all living things, is still much in the realm of theory. That boron and some others are absolutely essential has been established beyond doubt, and some food chemists are now predicting that forty or even fifty traces are going to be found necessary for complete development in both plants and animals.

Then there are the vitamins. No discussion of foods could be complete without a word about vitamins. Natural vitamins, that is. Vitamins are the products of plants, but they seem to be more vital to correct bodily function in animals than they are in plants, where they practically all originate. Vitamins are not food, but like the enzymes with which they are usually associated, they have much to do with the correct digestion and assimilation of foods. Animals fed from a dynamic soil receive an abundance of natural vitamins—if the feed is not injured in some way through processing or is not devitalized by becoming stale. That is why, to get an ample supply of natural vitamins, one should consume an abundance of selected raw vegetables and fruits, and also see that cooking, when cooking is necessary, is carried out promptly and properly.

Vitamins are one of Nature's health factors, and they

are found at their best in products which are grown on well-balanced soils. Our present trouble is not the production of natural vitamins of high quality, but rather the still unsolved problem of preservation. Preservatives are more likely than not to destroy the vitamins rather than to preserve them.

11

Résumé

NEWLY built land, no matter how correct the fertilizing materials employed, is far from being a quality soil. Such land contains the makings of a quality soil, but, like an unbaked cake in the batter stage, it is still short of the "baking." This soil is still in the raw and it will remain in that condition until it has been processed by the various agents in the soil's workshop. From the practical angle, there is little the farmer can do about this final transformation of the raw materials into a soil ready for quality production. The soil agents will take their own time completing their tasks.

Right here is where many quality-food enthusiasts are skating on thin ice, especially with their salad crops and potherbs and some other types of greens. Some gardeners take produce from land that has been treated with undecayed barnyard manure or poultry manure only a short time before planting the crop. Such products are no more safely edible than produce harvested from a Chinese garden fertilized with "night soil." Sorry, gardeners, but those are facts!

Never should quick-growing crops, whose stems and

leaves are consumed as food, be grown on raw manure. Another thing: although the products grown on newly made land may be safe, these crops have been stimulated into *false growth,* to a certain extent. Don't let the superficial evidence of the crop deceive you. The growth on "unprocessed soil" may be vigorous and pleasing to the eye, but the high quality will not be there, irrespective of what a chemical analysis may reveal. This is owing to the fact that many factors connected with food quality are intangible. Both aroma and taste will at times tell more about food quality than a chemical analysis—if you can interpret these subtle signs. But body responses are even more certain. If the quality is in the food, it will manifest itself if the food is consumed for a reasonable length of time. And the reverse is equally true when the food is of low quality.

The only organic materials that should ever be applied to land from which quickly grown food crops are to be harvested is complete compost, or animal manures not less than two years old and completely decayed. Other undecayed plant refuse is safe enough from the health standpoint, but in requiring the soil agents to work on this coarse stuff, the gardener invites the neglect of his crops—if crops are growing on the land at that time—on the part of the soil workers, thereby lowering the quality of the produce. The soil agents cannot put quality into food while they are forced to do the work of scavengers. Provide them with the correct materials for building quality food, and they will build quality food, but not otherwise. The same rule applies to the production of quality ornamentals. Too often Nature's workers in the soil are asked to do the impossible.

Why not be guided by Nature's blueprint? In the temperate zone Nature adds materials to her soils in late summer and autumn. When the spring growing period arrives, only the later stages of disintegration are going on. The soil agents can therefore do their very best work with growth. That is a basic reason why wild greens are often more nutritious than cultivated crops. Even in the tropics there are growing and resting periods during which these same laws of Nature operate. Every jungle native knows exactly when his wild herbs are at their best. His reasons may be saturated with superstition, but he knows quality herbs as a bee knows choice blossoms.

How long it will take the agents of the soil to complete the processing of the raw materials in new, man-made land, will depend upon moisture, temperature, and the length of the working seasons. A safe rule is never to expect quality produce the first year following a complete land treatment when the materials have been applied during the spring or early summer. And don't expect anything approaching maximum-quality, health-carrying produce short of three years, and then only when there is continuous replacement of the right kinds of plant foods year after year. This does not mean heavy applications of the organics, nor does it apply to mineral applications. The latter should be put into the soil only when their need is definite, which is not annually.

And commercial chemicals? Unless used with caution and correctly, chemicals will lower food quality in a hurry. Some years ago a food lecturer came onto the platform carrying two bundles of carrots, one containing beautiful, large roots, the other knotty and scrawny ones. The lecturer explained that she had just analyzed two specimens from each bundle, and that the knotty roots showed a fair quality content. But with a gesture of impatience she tossed the larger roots on the table. "Every time I look at those fakes—for according to chemical analysis that is exactly what they are—I am reminded of a certain Biblical statement, 'Whited sepulchres full of all uncleanness!' And they sell us such vegetables and call them food!" In passing, the lecturer informed us that she had purchased the large carrots in a public market, but the others she had "borrowed" from a neglected farm garden. Chemicals had brought about a forced growth that had resulted in a good-looking product but with low food quality. Had the market gardeners employed a correct combination of the natural and the chemical, the lecturer's report could have been much different.

Once I attended a flower exhibit that was a picture of garrish beauty. The cluster arrangements were without exception the work of skilled artists. From the point of mechanics, there was absolutely nothing more to be desired. Even so, as I moved from one gorgeous attraction to another, I felt much as a sensitive musician must feel when he hears Beethoven played on a piano out of tune. Despite the superficial perfection, the extraordinary size of some specimens, and their dazzling brilliance, I missed at every turn the pleasing effects that radiate from a cluster of *natural* blooms.

I sensed my own disappointment when, near one end of the long hall, I came upon a large bowl of mixed flowers, the old-fashioned hardy blooms so familiar to most of us. But hardy and vigorous though they were, these flowers carried quality in size, structure, and color. As I stood there and gazed at the mass of handsome colors, my sense of disappointment quickly left me. The arrangement of the flowers left much to be desired, but it was the strength of character, the mellowness of color in the exhibit that was so overpowering. No garrishness, even though there was poor arrangement; and clearly no forcing for the special occasion of this flower show. Here, simply, was Nature at her natural best, able evidence that the soil in which the flowers had been grown possessed the natural vigor for a sublime result. A blue ribbon swung from a sturdy stem at the top of which rested a huge zinnia.

Flower-forcing is entirely legitimate and even essential in commercial floriculture. I would be the last to condemn it, because the public desires it. Commercial growers probably could not otherwise supply the demands made upon them. And a forced blossom, unlike a forced vegetable, does have merits that should not be ignored. And yet, natural methods of growing are often ignored when greater adherence to them could do wonders for quality. A rhythmic soil has possibilities beyond the reach of any artificial treatment. Maximum size is not only possible the natural way, but much more goes along with it: a satisfying sense of harmony on the part of the gardener with conditions as they were intended to be.